W9-CRN-851

Childcraft

THE HOW AND WHY LIBRARY

VOLUME 6

The Green Kingdom

World Book, Inc.

a Scott Fetzer company

Chicago London Sydney Toronto

World Book, Inc.
525 West Monroe
Chicago, IL 60606

© 1990, 1989, 1987, 1986, 1985 by World Book, Inc. © 1982,
1981, 1980, 1979 U.S.A. by World Book-Childcraft International,
Inc. © 1976, 1974, 1973, 1971, 1970, 1969, 1968, 1965, 1964
U.S.A. by Field Enterprises Educational Corporation.
International Copyright © 1987, 1986, 1985 by World Book, Inc.
International Copyright © 1982, 1981, 1980, 1979 by World Book-
Childcraft International, Inc.
International Copyright © 1976, 1974, 1973, 1971, 1970, 1969,
1968, 1965, 1964 by Field Enterprises Educational Corporation.

ISBN 0-7166-0191-5
Library of Congress Catalog Card Number 90-70178
Printed in the United States of America
A/IA

Acknowledgments

The publishers of Childcraft—The How and Why Library gratefully
acknowledge the courtesy of the following publishers, persons,
and organizations for permission to use copyrighted poems,
excerpts from poems, and special illustrations appearing in
this volume. Full illustration acknowledgments appear
on pages 278-279.

"The Florist Shop," by Rachel Field. From Taxis and Toadstools by
Rachel Field, copyright 1926 by Doubleday & Company, Inc.
Reprinted by permission of the publisher and World's Work Ltd.

"Four Seasons," by Rowena Bastin Bennett. Reprinted by
permission of the author.

"Maytime Magic," by Mabel Watts. Reprinted by permission of
the author.

"Mists of Daybreak," by Yosa Buson. From A Year of Japanese
Epigrams, edited and translated by William N. Porter and published
by Oxford University Press.

"Night," by Sara Teasdale. Excerpt reprinted with permission of
The Macmillan Company from Collected Poems by Sara Teasdale.
Copyright 1930 by Sara Teasdale Filsinger, renewed 1958 by
Guaranty Trust Company of New York, Executor.

"Package of Seeds," by Aileen Fisher. Reprinted from I Wonder
How, I Wonder Why, ©1962 by Aileen Fisher, by permission of
Abelard-Schuman, Ltd. All rights reserved.

"So This Is Autumn," by W. W. Watt, from One Man's Meter by
W. W. Watt. Copyright © 1959 by W. W. Watt. Reprinted by
permission of Holt, Rinehart and Winston, Inc.

"Tomato Time," by Myra Cohn Livingston. From The Moon and a
Star and Other Poems, © 1965 by Myra Cohn Livingston. Reprinted
by permission of Marian Reiner for the author.

Photograph from Island Life by Sherwin Carlquist, © 1965 by
Sherwin Carlquist. Reproduced by permission of Doubleday &
Company, Inc.

Volume 6

The Green Kingdom

Contents

Seasons of Life

Springtime is a green time
*   When seedlings start their growing.*
Summertime's a rainbow time
*   When many blooms are blowing.*
Autumntime's a brown time
*   When seeds are ripe for sowing;*
But wintertime's a white time
*   (It is the flowers' nighttime)*
When stars of frost are glowing.

FOUR SEASONS
Rowena Bastin Bennett

Sleeping life

It is the flowers' nighttime . . .

In many parts of the world it is winter, and the ground lies cold and hard beneath snow and frost. The sleeping trees are brown and bare. The dry, dead stems of last year's plants shiver in the cold wind.

But under the snow and in the frozen ground are millions of seeds, underground stems, and roots that will be next summer's plants. Each seed is a package of life, with a tiny plant and a store of food inside it. On the roots and stems are buds, and each bud is the heart of a sleeping plant. A little warmth, a taste of water, and the plants will awake again.

And down in the ground, or snuggled beneath the snow-covered leaves, summer animals—chipmunks, frogs, ants, spiders —are sleeping, too. Like the plants, the animals are also waiting for warmth and life to come back to the land.

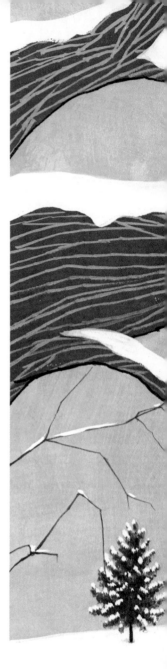

Wake-up time

The winter months slide slowly by. The sun begins to shine a little longer each day. The air grows a little warmer. The snow begins to melt and soak into the ground. The earth grows warm and wet and soft. This is what the plants have been waiting for.

Water soaks into the seeds. Their hard covers grow soft. The water makes the tiny plants and the stores of food inside the seeds swell up. The plants burst out of the seeds. From each seed, a tiny root pushes down into the earth, and a tiny stem with one or two leaves springs up.

The sleeping buds and roots of the older plants begin to stir. There is water in the ground again for them to find and drink.

Plants aren't the only things stirring. It is now wake-up time for many of the sleeping animals, too.

The world turns green

Now the tiny green heads of new plants are poking up from the brown earth and around the patches of snow. The little plants hold out their tiny leaves toward the sun. Their roots push down and spread out in the ground.

The roots of the older plants are working, too. They take in water. The water goes up through the plant and into the new little leaves.

The land is turning green, and green means food for many animals. So now the animals begin to appear.

Once again, plants and animals, the two kinds of living things, begin life anew in the springtime.

A world full of life

The days grow longer. The air is warm and the ground is filled with water. The new plants are shooting up. They twist and turn and stretch as they grow. They reach for as much sunlight as they can get. Their leaves grow to full size. Many of them have flowers. Many of the trees and other plants have flowers, too.

Animals of all kinds are everywhere. Many of them are laying eggs or having babies. It is the beginning of summer.

A butterfly and a buttercup

A butterfly belongs to the Animal Kingdom. A buttercup belongs to the Plant Kingdom. The butterfly moves through the air. The buttercup is rooted in the ground. They seem very different from each other. But are they?

Butterflies and most other animals come from eggs. And so do buttercups and most plants. A plant's egg and the part of the plant around it grow into a seed—a tiny plant and a store of food. The inside of a butterfly egg grows into a tiny, curled-up caterpillar and a store of food.

A caterpillar hatches from an egg and begins to eat. A buttercup sprouts from a seed and begins to make food for itself. Both the caterpillar and the buttercup must have food, water, and air to live. So must all plants and animals.

A caterpillar grows. So does a buttercup. The caterpillar changes into a brightly colored butterfly. The buttercup bursts out with bright little flowers. When these things happen, both the butterfly and the buttercup have reached an important part of their lives. The butterfly will mate and lay eggs. The buttercup flowers will grow seeds. The butterfly eggs will become new little caterpillars. And the buttercup seeds will become new little buttercup plants.

So a butterfly and a buttercup aren't so different after all. Plants and animals both have the same needs and they both do many of the same things. They are both living things, each with its own way of life.

Plants at work

During the warm summer months all the plants work to stay alive and to make new life. Their roots take in water. Their leaves make food. Their flowers make seeds.

As the seeds grow, the flower petals wither away and drop off. Soon, nothing is left of each flower but the little swelling where the seeds are growing.

As the warm days pass, the swellings begin to change. They become something different on each kind of plant. They become berries, or nuts, or other kinds of fruits. Inside the fruits are the seeds.

These seeds must now go traveling. Some will float through the air on leafy wings or silky parachutes. Others have spikes that catch hold of an animal's fur. Some will be dropped in far places by birds and animals that ate the fruits the seeds were in. In each seed a tiny new plant waits to begin its life next spring.

When the plants make their seeds, it's a good time for the animals. Many of the seeds and berries and pods and fruits are good to eat. The animals that sleep during winter can now fatten up for their long nap. Others can fill their underground houses with food for the winter.

Settling down to sleep

By the end of summer the plants have done their work. They have made their seeds and sent them out to find new growing places.

For many plants, life is now over. But the trees and other plants that have longer lives are getting ready for winter. They have dropped all their leaves. The ground is growing cold and hard. Soon there will be no water for roots to find. Once again they must sleep until spring arrives.

The animals, too, are getting ready for winter. Many of the birds and insects have flown away to warmer places. Many of the animals that have stayed behind have already gone to sleep.

The green earth is turning brown. In a few weeks, snowflakes will come spinning out of the sky. The land will turn white.

It is the flowers' nighttime . . .

Plant Ways

Have you ever wondered why leaves change color in the fall? Or why some flowers smell nice and some don't? Or what pine cones are for? Do you know why some trees stay green all winter? Why tree bark is rough? What flowers do?

The next few pages answer questions you may have asked about plants. Some of the answers will surprise you!

Now far and near on field and hill
We watch the death of chlorophyll
As earl autumn rushes in
With xanthophyll and carotin.
I hold that ignorance is bliss
Considering the fact that this
Is how a botanist perceives
The colorings of autumn leaves.

So This Is Autumn
W. W. Watt

Spanish needle

touch-me-not

wheat

How a seed grows

The seed bursts open.
Out comes a tiny root.

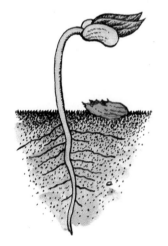

As the root grows down,
the stem pushes up.

The first leaves begin to
make food for the plant.

What's in a seed?

A seed is a baby plant and a bundle of food all wrapped up in a package.

Different kinds of plants have different kinds of seeds. Some seeds are as big as a baseball. Others are smaller than a grain of sand. Some are round, some are flat, some are long and thin. But in every kind of seed a baby plant, with its store of food, is waiting to grow.

Springtime is come-to-life time for seeds that have been in the earth all winter. Water from melting snow and soft spring rains sinks into the earth and soaks into

Seeds come in many different shapes and sizes. The seeds shown in these pictures are the same sizes and shapes as the real seeds.

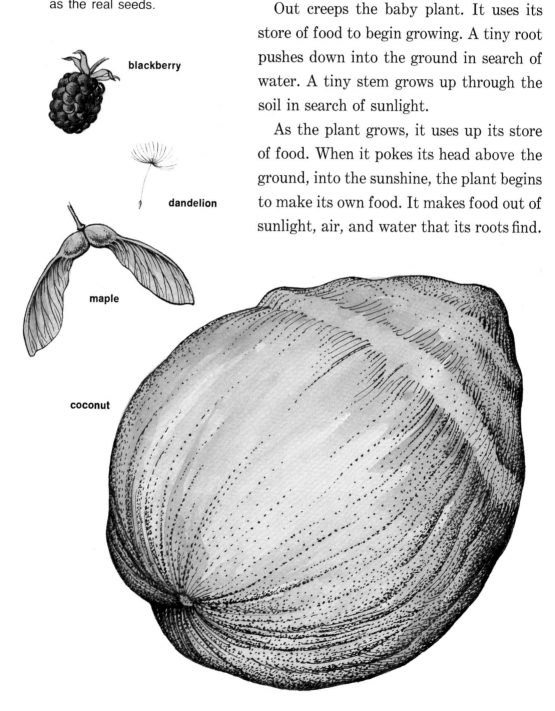

blackberry

dandelion

maple

coconut

the seed. The seed's tough shell—the cover of the package—becomes soft. The food inside the shell swells up with water. Then the shell bursts open.

Out creeps the baby plant. It uses its store of food to begin growing. A tiny root pushes down into the ground in search of water. A tiny stem grows up through the soil in search of sunlight.

As the plant grows, it uses up its store of food. When it pokes its head above the ground, into the sunshine, the plant begins to make its own food. It makes food out of sunlight, air, and water that its roots find.

Do all plants come from seeds?

Some plants do not come from seeds. They come from spores.

A spore is usually made up of one cell—a tiny bag of living jelly that you would need a microscope to see. Spores have a covering on the outside to protect them.

Spores grow in little sacks on the leaves and stems of mosses, ferns, horsetails, and some other plants. There are usually a great many spores in each sack, but very few of the spores will become new plants.

woodland ferns

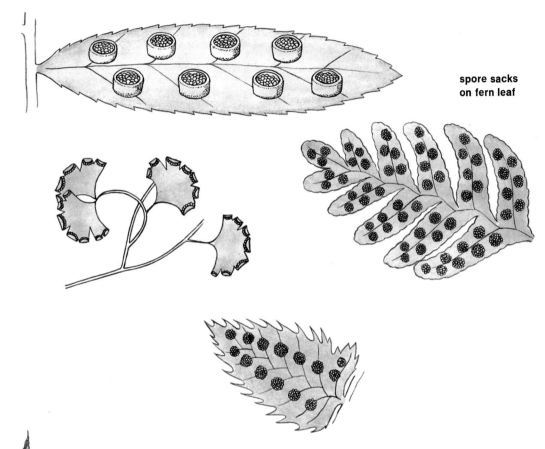

**spore sacks
on fern leaf**

These spores are blown into the air and float away on the wind. Out of millions of them, only a few come down where there is the right kind of soil, water, and light they need if they are to grow.

A spore grows into a tiny green plant that is nothing at all like the plant the spore came from. But this tiny plant makes cells that join together. These cells then grow into plants that are just like the plant the spore came from.

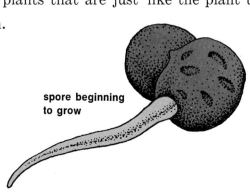

**spore beginning
to grow**

Why leaves are green

In the furry, finny, feathered world of the animal kingdom, there are many different colors. There are orange and brown giraffes, white polar bears, blue beetles, and red birds. But in the plant world—the green kingdom—the leaves of nearly all plants are just one color—green. Why?

The biggest difference between plants and animals is that animals eat and plants don't. Plants are able to make their own food. Leaves have a wonderful stuff inside them that makes food out of air and water, with the help of sunshine. This wonderful stuff is called chlorophyll. And chlorophyll is green.

So a leaf is green because it is filled with chlorophyll. And chlorophyll makes food for the plant.

Animals have no chlorophyll. They can't make food inside themselves as plants can. Neither can you. But wouldn't it be fun if you could? You would always be full and you'd never have to chew!

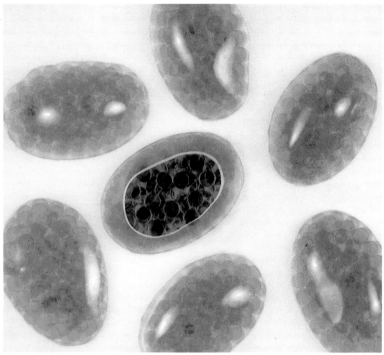

chlorophyll

Inside a leaf are millions of tiny packages filled with green stuff called chlorophyll. All these green packages give the leaf its green color.

Sunlight passes through the clear skin of the leaf.

Air enters the leaf through tiny openings called stomata.

Water passes along the stem and into the leaf.

What leaves do

Leaves don't seem to do anything at all. But if you could become tiny enough to peek *inside* a leaf—you would have a surprise!

Sunlight comes into a leaf through the leaf's skin, which is clear like glass. Beneath the skin are millions of tiny "bags" called cells. These cells are like little balloons filled with water and living jelly. Inside the cells are small green packages called chloroplasts. The chloroplasts are green-colored because they are filled with a green stuff called chlorophyll. The chlorophyll catches some of the sunlight that falls on a leaf.

While the green packages are catching sunlight, other things are happening in the leaf. Air comes into the leaf through many tiny openings. Water, moving up from the roots far below, flows through the leaf. The air and water mix together and flow into the cells.

These cells are like little food factories. Here, the green chlorophyll works away. Using sunlight for energy, it changes water and a gas from the air (called carbon dioxide) into sugar. Some of this sugar is used as food for the plant. Some of it is mixed with minerals from the ground and is changed to other kinds of food.

So, all summer long, leaves are doing what leaves do best—making food.

The sugars are the plant's food. They are stored in these cells.

cells and chloroplasts

A leaf is made up of tiny "bags" called cells. Inside the cells are green packages called chloroplasts, where food is made.

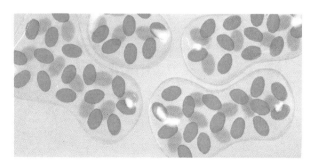

Why leaves change color in autumn

Inside a leaf there are millions of tiny packages of color—yellow, orange, and green. The yellow is called xanthophyll, the orange is carotene, or carotin, and the green is chlorophyll. The green color covers up the others, and that's why leaves are green all summer.

Near the end of summer, the green chlorophyll fades and disappears. Then the yellow xanthophyll and orange carotene can be seen. That's why many leaves turn yellow and orange in autumn.

All summer, water goes into each leaf through tiny tubes in the leaf's stem. Leaves make sugar, which is a plant's food. Sap carries the sugar out of the leaf to other parts of the plant. Near summer's end, a thin layer of cork grows over the tubes and seals them up. No more water can get into the leaf. Sugar often gets trapped inside leaves when the tubes are sealed up. This sugar may cause the sap to turn red or purple and make the leaves look red or purple.

When leaves are dry and dead, they turn brown.

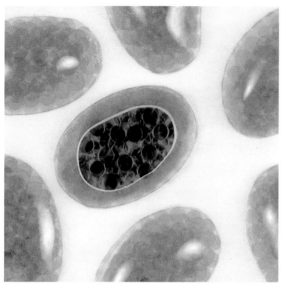

chloroplasts in summer

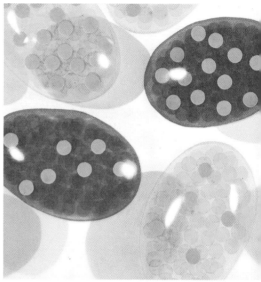

chloroplasts in autumn

Inside each leaf cell are tiny "packages" called chloroplasts. They are filled with colors. But, in summer, one color—green—covers up all the other colors.

In autumn, the green color in the chloroplasts slowly fades away. Then you can see the other colors. This is why leaves change color in autumn.

What roots do

Roots are like sponges. They soak up water. And roots are anchors, too.

A plant's roots grow down into the earth. They spread out and send out branches. They curve around stones. They grow toward damp places in search of water.

There is usually lots of water in the ground from rain that has soaked in. Mixed with the water are iron, copper, and other minerals. Plants need minerals to

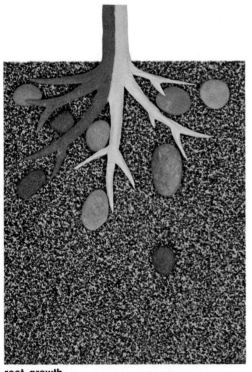
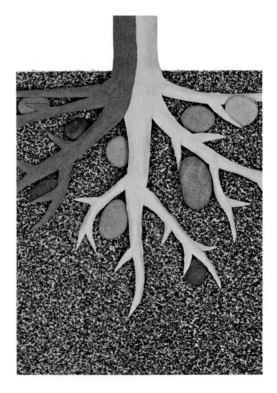

root growth

A plant's roots grow down into the earth. They send out branches that spread out and curve around stones.

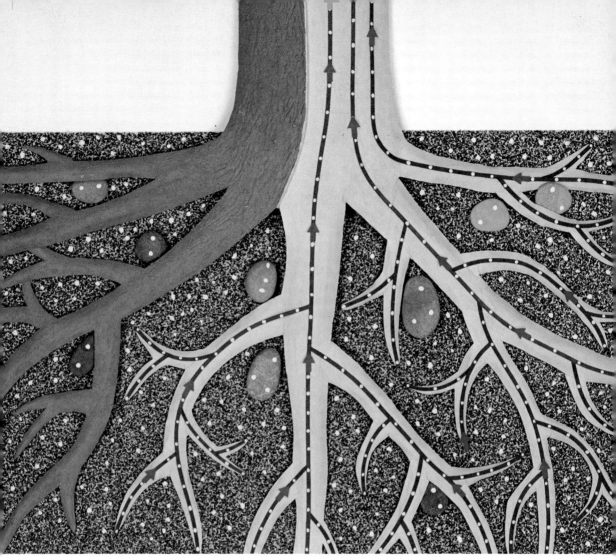

roots taking in water

Roots take water (dots) from the soil.
Arrows show water moving up the trunk.

stay healthy. Roots soak minerals up along with water, and send them to all parts of the plant.

Besides getting what the plant needs from the soil, roots do something else, too. By growing down and spreading out in the ground, they hold a plant tightly in place. Strong winds can't blow the plant away. Floods of rain can't wash it away. It is held in place by its root anchors.

Why some trees lose their leaves in autumn

Many trees that live where winters are freezing cold lose their leaves each fall.

Leaves make the food that keeps a tree alive. But to make food, and to stay alive themselves, leaves need water. A tree gets water from the ground. The roots take it in and the leaves pull it up through the trunk.

In late summer, a thin layer of cork grows where each leaf's stem is attached to the twig. Water can no longer get into the leaves. They dry up and die.

In summer, a tree's roots take water (dots) from the soil. The red arrows show how water moves up the tree, into the leaves. Some goes out into the air.

Wind tears the dead leaves from the branches. There is no reason for a tree to keep its leaves in winter. There is no water for them. In winter, the water in the ground turns to ice. The roots can't take in this frozen water.

But in springtime, the ground warms up. The ice melts. Rain and melting snow fill the earth with water again. Then a tree's roots start taking in water and the tree grows new leaves.

In autumn, the tubes that bring water to the leaves close up. Without water the leaves die and fall. Water stays in the tree in winter, but doesn't move.

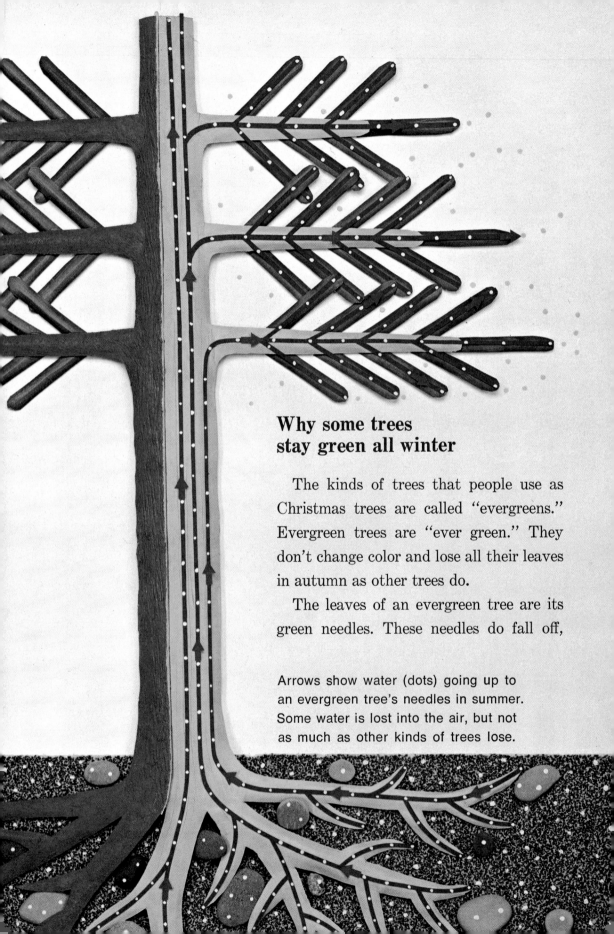

Why some trees stay green all winter

The kinds of trees that people use as Christmas trees are called "evergreens." Evergreen trees are "ever green." They don't change color and lose all their leaves in autumn as other trees do.

The leaves of an evergreen tree are its green needles. These needles do fall off,

Arrows show water (dots) going up to an evergreen tree's needles in summer. Some water is lost into the air, but not as much as other kinds of trees lose.

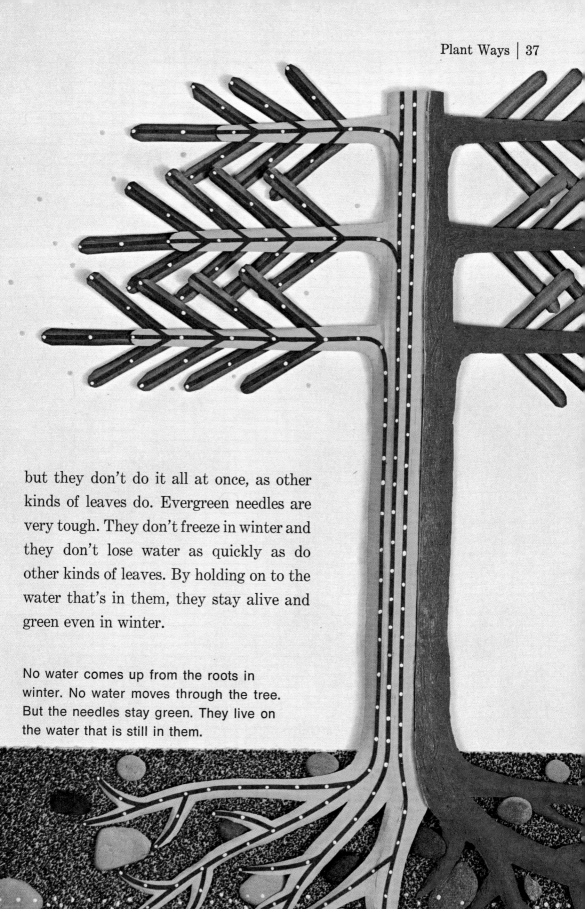

but they don't do it all at once, as other kinds of leaves do. Evergreen needles are very tough. They don't freeze in winter and they don't lose water as quickly as do other kinds of leaves. By holding on to the water that's in them, they stay alive and green even in winter.

No water comes up from the roots in winter. No water moves through the tree. But the needles stay green. They live on the water that is still in them.

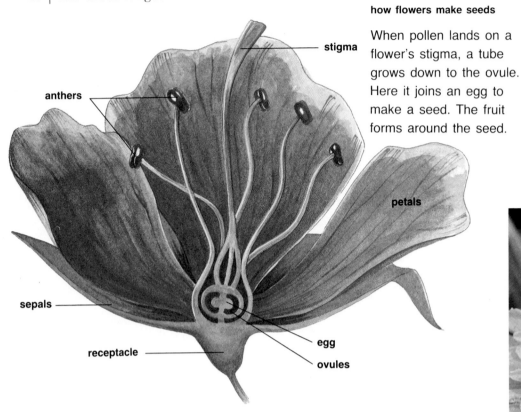

stigma

anthers

petals

sepals

receptacle

egg

ovules

how flowers make seeds

When pollen lands on a flower's stigma, a tube grows down to the ovule. Here it joins an egg to make a seed. The fruit forms around the seed.

What a flower does

A flower's job is to make seeds.

The stigma, which is often covered with a sticky fluid, is in the middle of a flower. Around it are one or more tiny stems with knobs on top. These knobs are called anthers. Inside the anthers is a dust called pollen, which is usually golden.

For a flower to make seeds, pollen from one flower must fall on the stigma of the same kind of flower. A tiny tube then grows out of the pollen and pushes down into a part of the flower called the ovule. A tiny egg is in the ovule.

The ovule now grows into a seed. Inside the seed, the egg becomes a tiny plant. The fruit forms around the seed.

How some insects help flowers

All flowers are seed makers. But to make seeds, a flower must get some pollen from another flower like itself. Many flowers need the help of bees or other insects to bring pollen to them.

How do flowers get insects to visit them? Flowers make sweet juice called nectar, which many insects like. Flowers "advertise" their nectar. Their white or bright-colored petals and sweet scent tell insects that there is nectar.

Bees and other insects go to these flowers. To get the nectar, a bee pushes down into a flower. Some pollen from the flower's anthers falls on its body.

Then the bee buzzes to another flower and pushes down into it. Some pollen on the bee's body brushes off onto a part called a stigma, which is often sticky. When this happens, the flower may begin to make seeds.

bee spreading pollen

(above) Bees and other insects help flowers make seeds by carrying pollen from one flower to another. (left) Pollen from the anthers brushes off onto this bee's back.

Flowers that are pollinated by insects have bright colors and sweet smells to attract the insects.

salvia flower and bee

grass flowers

Flowers that are pollinated by the wind don't need bright colors or sweet smells.

Why some flowers smell nice— and some don't

Flowers that need the help of insects to make seeds have smells and bright colors. The smells and colors attract insects to the flowers. The insects carry pollen from one flower to another. Pollen helps make seeds.

Most flowers have sweet smells that attract bees and other insects that like sweet smells. Some plants, such as the skunk cabbage, have unpleasant smells to attract insects that like bad smells.

But some flowers don't need the help of insects. The pollen of these flowers is carried to other flowers by the wind. Since these flowers don't have to attract insects, they don't need bright colors or smells. They are usually small and greenish or brownish and grow in tight bunches. You can see such flowers on grass.

What pine cones do

The pine tree is an evergreen tree with needles for leaves. The pine tree has pine cones, which are its seed makers.

There are two kinds of pine cones. One is small and delicate. It is full of tiny grains of pollen that look like yellow powder. The wind blows the pollen out of the cones.

The other kind of cone is covered with wood scales. These look somewhat like the scales on a fish. At the bottom of each scale are two little things called ovules, which contain eggs. The wind brings pollen grains to the ovules. If a grain of pollen reaches an ovule, the ovule grows into a seed.

Each pine seed has a woody wing, and when the seed is ripe the wind blows it off the scale. When it reaches the ground, the seed may take root and grow into a new pine tree.

pollen-carrying cones

seed-carrying cone

insect galls on oak leaf

Why some leaves have bumps

Sometimes, the leaves or stems of plants become spotted with little greenish or yellowish-white bumps. These bumps are called galls. They are often made when an insect lays eggs on very young stems or leaves. The insect eggs cause a change in the growing plant. The change makes little swellings grow up around the eggs.

Some galls look like beads, some look like marbles, some look like balls of pink cotton. The shape of a gall tells what kind of insect made it. The baby insect is protected by having the gall around it. And the baby insect uses the inside of the gall for food.

When insects lay eggs on leaves, little bumps called galls swell up all around the eggs.

Why tree bark is rough

Bark is a tree's skin.

It is tough and hard and protects the soft, inside part of the tree.

A tree trunk grows from the inside out. Each year, a ring of new, soft wood grows around the trunk, inside the bark. This makes the trunk get thicker. The old, hard bark can't stretch as the tree gets thicker—it cracks and splits and crumbles away to powder to make room for the new wood. That's why a tree's bark always looks rough and cracked and bumpy.

As each ring of new wood grows, the outside of the ring becomes young bark. A tree is always making new bark and shedding its old bark.

Some trees, such as the beech, have smooth bark. These trees grow slowly. Their bark grows as they grow, and so the bark doesn't crack and split.

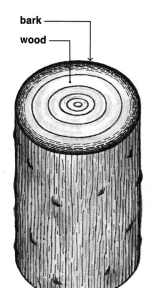

bark

wood

bark

wood

young and old bark

Tree bark grows from the inside.
As new bark forms, old bark on
the outside cracks and falls off.

Do plants ever move?

Plants are moving all the time. But they move so slowly we just don't notice these movements.

Instead of moving from one place to another, as animals do, plants move by growing. As a plant grows, it twists and stretches, turning its leaves to the light.

Some vines wind around a tree as they grow. Other vines, such as the grape or sweet pea, grow little arms called tendrils. These little arms reach out and wrap themselves around sticks or poles that people put nearby to help the vines grow.

Many flowers move their petals. They open them wide in the morning and close them tight at night. The leaves of some plants do this, too.

day lily

As the sun begins to rise, the day lily flower begins to open.

Moving very slowly, the day lily petals open.

Some plants have seeds and fruits that move. The witch hazel shoots its seeds out when they are ripe. The slim, dry fruit of porcupine grass has a long, sharp, twisted tail. In wet weather, when the ground is soft, the tail untwists and pushes the sharp, pointed fruit into the ground.

A jumping bean is a plant seed that seems to move by itself. But it doesn't, really. One kind of moth lays its eggs in the beans—one egg in each bean. The egg hatches into a little caterpillar that uses the inside of the bean for food. Sometimes the caterpillar hooks its legs into the bean and jerks its body as hard as it can. This is what makes the bean hop.

It has taken the day lily an hour and a half to open this much.

After about three hours, the day lily is all the way open.

Why a plant wilts

Have you ever seen fire fighters using a fire hose? The hose looks stiff and fat while water is running through it. But when the fire is over and the fire fighters turn off the water, the empty hose is limp.

A plant is somewhat like a fire hose. As long as a plant's roots keep pumping water into it, the plant's stems and leaves stand up straight and stiff. But if the plant doesn't get enough water to stay filled, it will soon flop over, just like an empty fire hose.

Can plants see, or hear, or feel?

A sunflower seems to watch the sun. It slowly turns its flower head as the sun moves across the sky. Can a sunflower see?

If you touch the leaves of a plant called the sensitive plant, they will suddenly fold up and droop. Then, in a short time, they will unfold and straighten up again. Can the sensitive plant feel?

Scientists say that no plant can really see or hear or feel. But plants *are* living creatures that twist and turn to move toward sunlight or away from heat. Most plants do this so slowly we don't notice it. But some plants, such as the sensitive plant, move quickly. This makes it seem as if they can feel. But plants don't have brains or nerves. So they probably can't feel pain the way you do.

Before the leaves of the sensitive plant are touched, they are wide open. But when the plant is touched, its leaves suddenly fold up and droop.

sensitive plant

Nature's Neighbors

Do you know that plants live in communities just as people do?

A forest is a plant community of many trees. A pond is a community of many water plants. Prairies, deserts, and oceans are plant communities, too.

Plants live in places that have the kind of weather and soil they need. Plants in a swamp grow best in a wet place. Plants in a desert grow best in a very dry place. Swamp plants and desert plants could never be neighbors.

Communities of plants and animals are called biomes. Every plant, animal, and person lives in some kind of biome. You can find out what kind you live in from the next few pages.

Where the plants change their clothes

Do the trees where you live change their clothes during the year? Do they wear light green buds in the springtime, dark green leaves in the summer, and beautiful reds, golds, and purples in the fall? If they do, you live in the woodland community.

Trees—oaks, maples, elms, lindens, beeches, and many others—are the most important plants in the woodland. Once, these trees grew together in huge forests in many parts of the world. Most of these forests have been cut down. But if any of these kinds of trees grow near you, you're probably living where a great woodland forest once grew, long ago.

Most of the plants in the woodland grow leaves and flowers in spring and summer. These kinds of plants grow best where summers aren't too hot and winters aren't too cold, and where the ground receives just about the same amount of moisture all year round.

woodland community

Oak, maple, and hickory trees
are common in the woodland.

Plants of the woodland community

hepaticas

skunk cabbages

wake robin

black walnut tree

sugar maple tree

Life in the woodlands

In the woodland community there are four seasons.

In spring, little wild flowers are the first to bloom. Then trees and bushes bud. Birds appear and build nests. From spring until the end of summer, the woodland is filled with birds, squirrels, rabbits, and many other little animals.

In fall, the leaves change color. Most birds fly south for winter. Snakes, turtles, frogs, many insects, and some of the furry animals hibernate. But, if the winter is mild, birds, rabbits, and other animals stay active.

Giant lawns

Grass doesn't need as much water as trees and bushes do. So grass grows well in wide, flat places that are too dry for trees but not dry enough to be deserts. These places are like giant lawns. They are called grasslands or prairies.

The grass on a grassland may be short, middle-sized, or tall, depending on how much moisture there is. Hardly any trees

grassland community

Grasses and small plants with white or colored flowers are neighbors in a grassland.

or bushes grow on a grassland, but there are many small plants with white or colored flowers.

Big herds of sheep or cattle graze on many grasslands. Other grasslands have been turned into farmland where wheat and corn are raised. Wheat and corn grow well in a grassland because they themselves are grasses.

Plants of the
grassland community

gray-headed coneflowers

red top grass

pampas grass

purple prairie
clover

Indian
grass

rattlesnake grass

Life in the grasslands

Most big animals that live on grasslands, such as zebras, eat grass. Most small animals, such as rabbits, eat plant leaves and seeds. There are also meat-eating animals—foxes, snakes, and, in some places, lions and leopards.

Many meat-eating birds, such as hawks, go hunting on grasslands. They swoop down to catch rabbits and other small animals.

It's hard for a hunted animal to hide on grasslands. The ground is low and flat and there are few trees or bushes. Many animals crouch down and hide. Some, such as rabbits and zebras can save themselves by running. And some, such as these prairie dogs, dig tunnels in which to hide.

Plants that like wet feet

Cats don't like wet feet. But the plants called cattails do. And so do many other kinds of plants. So these plants often live together in ponds, lakes, and rivers.

Cattails, bulrushes, and bur reeds live along the edges of streams and ponds, with their roots and parts of their stems underwater. Water lilies live a little farther out, with their leaves and flowers floating on the water. Pondweeds may live even farther out, and often are completely under the water.

And some plants, such as the tiny duckweed, have no stems at all. They float on top of the water like little green rafts, and their roots hang down into the water.

pond community

Cattails, bulrushes, and floating water lilies are often neighbors in a pond such as this.

Plants of ponds, lakes, and rivers

lotuses

arrowhead

duckweed

papyrus

bulrushes

water lilies

Life in ponds, lakes, and rivers

Plants that grow in and around ponds, lakes, and rivers give food and shelter to many animals.

Grebes and other water birds use these plants to make nests. Muskrats eat plants such as cattails and also use them for building houses. Frogs often fasten their eggs to water plants. And when the eggs hatch, the tadpoles use plants as food.

Bass and other big fish hide among the water plants. From these hiding places, they dart out to snap up careless frogs and small fish.

ocean community

Most ocean plants live in shallow water where they can get plenty of sunlight.

Underwater forests and meadows

Some plants live only in the salty water of the ocean. These plants live together in strange underwater forests and meadows.

Seaweeds live in shallow water near the shore, where they can get sunlight. They grow in great tangled bunches that hug the rocks to keep from being swept away by the crashing waves.

Eelgrass grows at the muddy bottom of shallow water along the edge of the shore. It looks like a lawn that needs mowing.

One of the strangest of all plants floats out in the middle of the ocean. It lives in a glassy shell that is a sort of box with a lid. This plant, called a diatom, is very tiny. There are billions and billions of them in the ocean. Diatoms are often called "the pasture of the sea." This is because these tiny ocean plants are the main food for many sea creatures.

a kelp forest

rockweed

Plants of the ocean
community

red-tongue seaweed

sea lettuce

sargassum

Life in the ocean

Diatoms are tiny plants that live in the ocean. They can be seen only with a microscope.

Diatoms are green plants, and make their own food. Tiny, shrimplike copepods eat them. Small fish eat copepods. And the small fish are eaten by bigger fish.

Without diatoms to eat, the copepods would die. Soon, all the other sea animals would die. You can see how important the tiny diatoms are!

The Christmas trees' home

In the northern parts of the world, winters are long and cold and summers are cool. This is where many of the trees people use as Christmas trees live.

There are huge forests of spruce trees, fir trees, and other evergreen trees in the northlands. These trees like cold weather. In winter, they are covered with snow. Then, in spring, the snow melts and soaks into the ground. This gives the trees most of the water they need.

Evergreen trees and plants are able to live in many parts of the world. But the cold northern forest communities are the real "cities" of the evergreen trees.

northern forest community

◀ Most trees in the northern forest are conifers—trees that have cones.

birch
tree

twinflower

Plants of the
northern forest
community

white spruce tree

red pine tree

Life in the northern forest

Evergreen trees grow close together in the northern forests. There are many ponds and lakes. Beavers, muskrats, moose, deer, and water birds live on the plants that grow around the water. Today the biggest cat that lives in these northern forests is the lynx.

In the winter, it snows heavily. Many birds fly south. Squirrels and bears take long naps. Other animals, such as the elk, stay awake and active all winter.

bunchberry

Where trees take lots of baths

Many kinds of trees grow best where it is always hot and where they get lots of shower baths from the rain. These trees live together in forests in hot parts of the world where it rains heavily all year around. So much rain falls on these forests that they are called rain forests.

Rain forest trees stay green all the time. And they are much taller than most other kinds of trees. They are so tall they keep the sunlight from reaching the floor of the forest, so few plants can grow there. But many kinds of vines and plants, such as orchids, live high up on the branches of the tall trees. Here they can get sunlight. And many kinds of animals live in and under the trees of a rain forest community.

rain forest community

In a rain forest the trees are huge, and vines are as thick as a man's leg. Many people live in rain forests around the world.

passionflower

Plants of the rain forest community

cannon-ball tree

bauhinia vine

acanthus flower

stinkhorn fungus

Life in the tropical rain forest

Life is always much the same in a rain forest. The trees are always green. It rains almost every day. The air is hot, night and day. Most animals live in the trees.

There are monkeys, tree snakes, and brightly colored birds. There are tree frogs and many kinds of tree-dwelling insects. In some rain forests, there are great apes such as the orangutan.

desert community

Desert plants are able to live
without much water.

Plants that like it hot and dry

A desert seems like a bad place for plants. In most deserts, the sun is burning hot, and there's little water. Yet, many plants do live in deserts—plants that have solved the problems of living in a hot, waterless place.

Water is a desert plant's first problem. The only water most desert plants get is from rain. But it doesn't rain often in a desert. And when it does, the ground quickly dries. So, many desert plants have roots that spread far out and grow close to the top of the ground. These roots can catch lots of water, right away.

Most desert plants store up all the water they can get. Some plants, such as a barrel cactus, can swell up to hold a lot of water. Before a rain, a barrel cactus may look like a gray lump. But after a rain it looks like a fat, green ball.

Many animals might eat desert plants to get the water in them. Some plants have solved that problem. They are covered with thousands of sharp thorns or needles that keep animals away.

The thorns and needles do another job. They cast shadows. A plant such as a cactus casts thousands of tiny shadows on itself and makes its own shade.

Welwitschia

Plants of the
desert community

beavertail cactus

Joshua tree

pincushion cacti

yuccas

aloe

candelabra cactus

Life in the desert

During the day, the desert looks lifeless. Most desert animals hide where they can escape the heat.

When the sun goes down, a desert quickly cools. Desert rodents look for seeds. Lizards hunt insects. Snakes hunt the rodents and lizards.

It sometimes rains in a desert. When it does, the desert bursts into bloom, for there are many seeds in most deserts. But almost all of these plants quickly wither and die.

Plants of the frozen north

Far in the north, on the edge of the great sea that reaches to the North Pole, there is a great, flat plain called the tundra. Most of the time this plain is bare and frozen. The days are dark and sunless.

But, for a short time during the year, there are sunny days. The tundra warms up and the ice melts. Water soaks into the ground. And then plants bloom!

tundra community

The tundra is a great frozen plain, far in the north.

Even during these warmer, sunny days, a fierce, terrible wind blows over the tundra. So only tough, sturdy plants that grow close to the ground can live in this community. These include mosses, lichens, and small, flowering plants. Most of the tundra is a treeless plain, but sometimes there are birch and willow trees no bigger than bushes.

Plants of the
tundra community

cottongrass

sorrel

bilberries

reindeer moss

willows

Life on the tundra

In summer, the tundra is filled with animals. Little lemmings and other animals eat leaves, roots, and seeds. They, in turn, are hunted and eaten by animals such as foxes.

Winter comes suddenly. The ground freezes. Snow piles up. Most animals leave, but some stay. Lemmings burrow into the ground and live on seeds they stored away. Herds of musk oxen move from place to place, scraping with their hoofs to find lichens beneath the snow.

mountainside communities

Forest, grassland, tundra, and even
desert communities may all be found
on a mountainside.

Plant communities on mountains

A mountain is like a little world. It has many kinds of plant communities, just as the world has.

The upper part of a very high mountain is like the North Pole. It's always covered with ice and snow. The sun doesn't warm such high places very much.

A little lower on a mountain, the sun gives warmth. In summer, the snow melts and many plants bloom. These small plants grow close to the ground. This keeps them from being ripped up by the fierce winds that howl around the tops of mountains.

A little farther down on a mountain is the timber line. That's the highest place where trees can grow on a mountain. Along the timber line, most trees are small and bent, and nearly all the same size.

Below the timber line, the trees grow taller and closer together and make a forest that covers the sides of a mountain. This part of a mountain is like the northern parts of the world. It's cold and snowy in winter and cool and dry in summer. That's the kind of place where evergreen trees can grow, but other kinds of trees can't. So the forest is an evergreen forest.

Toward the lower part of a mountain it's warmer, and other kinds of trees can grow. If a mountain is in a part of the world where lots of rain falls, the lower part will be covered with a forest. But if a mountain stands in a place where not much rain falls, the lower part will be a grassy meadow. The lower parts of some mountains are even deserts.

Engelmann spruce trees

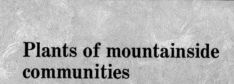

Plants of mountainside communities

edelweiss

mountain gentian

buttercups

fire lilies

aspen tree

Why tree-line trees are short

Every winter, snow covers the trees that grow near the tree line on mountains. The snow is about as deep one winter as the next.

When a tree is young, snow covers it each winter. But as it grows taller, the top will stick above the snow. Killed by the freezing winds that roar around the mountain, the top falls off.

In summer, the top grows again. In winter, it's killed. The tree can't grow taller than the deepest snow.

Strange and Surprising Plants

If you think that all plants are green, have leaves, and grow in the ground, you're in for a surprise.

Some plants are white, orange, or even purple, instead of green.

Some plants grow on bread, cheese, rocks, or even in trees, instead of in the ground.

Some plants look like animals, or even like rocks!

There are a great many kinds of the wonderful living things we call plants. And some of them are really strange and surprising!

mold growing on bread

When mold grows on bread,
it spoils the bread.

Plants that grow on bread and cheese

When a piece of bread gets old, it may become covered with pale, powdery spots. Each spot is a sort of "forest" of tiny, tiny plants called molds.

Molds, like all living things, are made of many tiny packages of life. These are called cells. But it takes only one cell to start a whole forest of mold. This kind of cell is called a spore.

A mold spore is smaller than a speck of dust. It floats in the air. When it lands on bread or something else it can use as food, it begins to grow by sending out many tiny threads. Some of these threads grow down, like roots. Others grow upward,

mold in Roquefort cheese

Some molds make the cheese
they grow in taste better.

like stems. Bunches of these threads make up the spots you see on moldy bread or cheese.

Some molds spoil food. But others make food taste better. Molds give such cheeses as Roquefort and Stilton their blue color and delicious flavor.

Molds grow on other things than bread and cheese. Some grow on plants. This usually spoils the plant.

Some molds grow on dead plants and animals. These molds help make dead things rot and break apart. They are part of nature's clean-up crew.

mold growing on a dead moth

Molds that make dead things rot, help make the soil richer.

mold growing on an orange

When mold grows on fruits or vegetables, it spoils them.

mold on raspberry jam

Mold often spoils food in cans or jars that have been opened.

yeast plants

Yeast plants are growing in the dough this
baker is mixing. The small photo shows how
growing yeast cells look under a microscope.

The baker's plant

If it weren't for a plant called yeast, we couldn't
have the kind of bread we eat.

Yeast plants don't look like plants. They look like
round drops of jelly. And they're so tiny you can see
them only with a microscope. They float in the air
everywhere. They don't do anything until they find a
warm, wet place where there's just the right kind of
food. And bread dough is just such a place.

Bread dough is made by mixing flour and water into
a warm, wet paste. To this is added sugar, which is
the yeast plants' favorite food. So when the yeast
plants get into bread dough, things start happening!

Here's what happens. When a yeast plant takes in

food, it swells up and splits into two new plants! Then, each new plant takes in food, swells up, and splits in two! Soon, there are millions of new yeast plants!

As all these tiny plants take in sugar, they change part of it to a gas. This gas causes many little bubbles to form inside the dough. This makes the dough swell up. When the dough is baked, all the bubbles fill with air. Then the bread is light and airy. But without yeast to change the sugar into gas, the dough won't swell up.

Long ago, people let the dough sit in a warm place so that yeast plants would get into it. Today, bakers don't have to wait for this to happen. They buy yeast in packages and mix it into the dough.

Grow a jar of yeast

You will need:
1 packet of yeast
1 tablespoon of sugar
about 3/4 cup of warm water
a glass jar

Dissolve the sugar in the water. Sprinkle the yeast on top. Leave the jar in a warm place.

As the yeast plants begin to use the sugar for food, the jar will fill with foam.

The yeast plants cause the foam by changing part of the sugar into carbon dioxide.

When the dough is baked, the bread is light and airy.

Chlamydomonas

Chlamydomonas is a tiny plant that swims like an animal!

Sometimes, 16 of these tiny plants form a jellylike wheel and live in it together.

Gonium

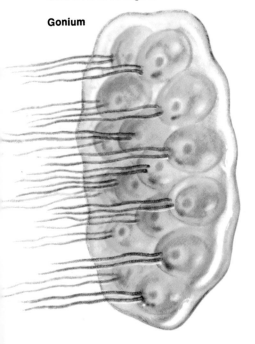

Plants that can swim!

If you peeked at a drop of pond water through a microscope, you'd be surprised! You would see many odd little creatures zipping about in the water.

One kind of creature looks like a green egg with two threads on one end. It has a red spot that's sort of an eye, for seeing light. And the creature swims by wiggling the threads. Is it an animal?

No, it's not an animal, even though it does move, as animals do. This green creature makes its own food, using sunlight, just as grass, trees, and other plants do. It's a plant—one of the plants we call algae.

Sometimes, 16 of these creatures fasten themselves together to make a sort of wheel. A kind of jellylike stuff holds them together. Each creature's two threads stick outside the wheel. When all the creatures wiggle their threads, the wheel rolls through the water!

And sometimes 32 of the creatures fasten themselves together into a ball. They keep their threads outside the ball and wiggle them to make the ball move, just like a bunch of men rowing a boat!

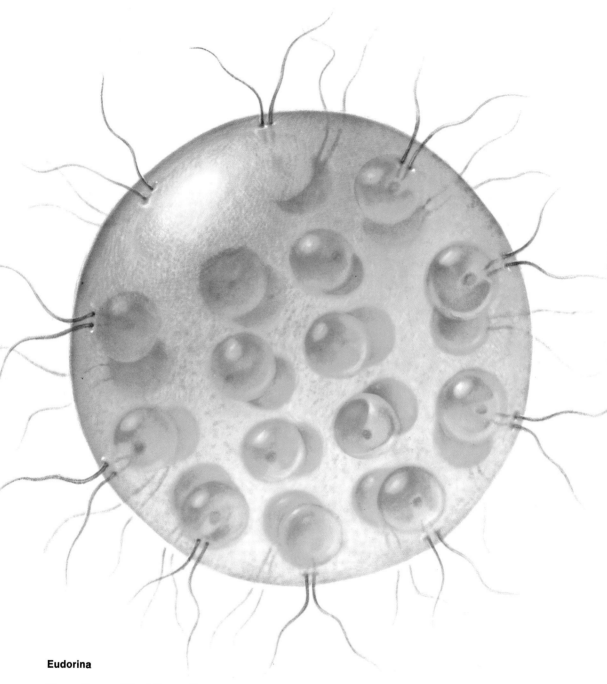

Eudorina

Sometimes, 32 of these tiny
plants form a jellylike ball
and live in it together.

Plants that trap insects

In many wet and swampy places there are plants that trap insects! But plants don't "eat." If plants don't "eat," then why do they catch insects?

All plants need a salt called a nitrate. It helps them grow. Most plants get this salt from the ground, but there isn't much of it in swamps. So some plants trap and digest insects to get the salt they need.

Plants that trap insects have different ways of catching them. The plant called a sundew has leaves that are covered with little hairs. On each hair there is a drop of sticky liquid. The sun sparkles on these drops and attracts insects. But when an insect touches one of the drops, it is stuck fast! Then, all the hairs around the insect bend over slowly. They push the insect down against the leaf. A juice oozes out of the leaf and slowly digests the insect!

The plant called a Venus's-flytrap works just like a trap. There are little hairs, like triggers, on each leaf. Around the edge of the leaf are little "claws." And each leaf can fold itself in half! When a fly or other insect lands on a leaf and touches one of the hair triggers, the leaf quickly folds in half. The little "claws" lock together and the insect is trapped. Then the plant digests it.

sundew

An aphid has been caught by the sticky hairs of the sundew plant.

(left) The open leaves of the Venus's-flytrap are ready to catch insects. (top) A fly lands on a leaf, touching a hair trigger. (above) The leaf closes, trapping an insect. Now the plant will slowly digest it.

Venus's-flytrap

pitcher plant

The butterwort traps insects much the same way the sundew does. The butterwort's leaves are sticky. When an insect crawls on a leaf, it gets stuck. Then the edges of the leaf curl in. The insect is pushed to the middle of the leaf, where juice oozes out and digests it.

The pitcher plant drowns insects! Its leaves are shaped like vases. They are usually half-filled with rain water. Inside the leaves are little pockets filled with a sweet-smelling juice. An insect crawls into a leaf to get at the juice. But the sides of the plant are slippery and covered with hairs that point downward. The

A fly has fallen into the pitcher plant's leaf. The leaf is like a vase filled with water. The fly will drown and the plant will digest it.

insect slides down the hairs and falls into the water. It drowns and is digested.

There is even a plant that catches worms! It catches them with a lasso, just as a cowboy catches a cow!

This plant is a fungus. It grows under the ground and is so small it can be seen only with a microscope. It spreads through the ground like many tiny threads. There are many loops in these threads.

Tiny worms, no bigger than the threads, crawl through the soil. When a worm crawls through a loop, the loop suddenly tightens! The worm is caught! Then the fungus digests it.

A tiny worm crawls among the threads of a fungus. There are loops in the threads.

The worm crawls through a loop. Suddenly the loop tightens and the worm is caught!

fungus and worm

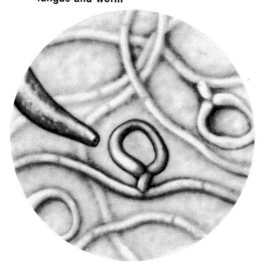

staghorn fern

Plants that live in trees

Do you know there are some kinds of plants that never grow in the ground? They grow high up in trees in tropical forests.

There's a good reason for this. In a forest where trees grow tall and close together, very little sunlight reaches the ground. The leaves block the sun. This makes it hard for other green plants to grow. They must have sunlight.

But orchids, Spanish moss, staghorn ferns, and many other plants get the sun they need by growing on the trunks and branches of trees. When it rains, their leaves and stems soak up and store water.

How do these plants get up into the trees? Most of them have light seeds that float in the wind. If one of these seeds is blown into a good spot in a tree it takes root. It spends the rest of its life there, hanging on.

wild pineapple

orchids

Spanish moss

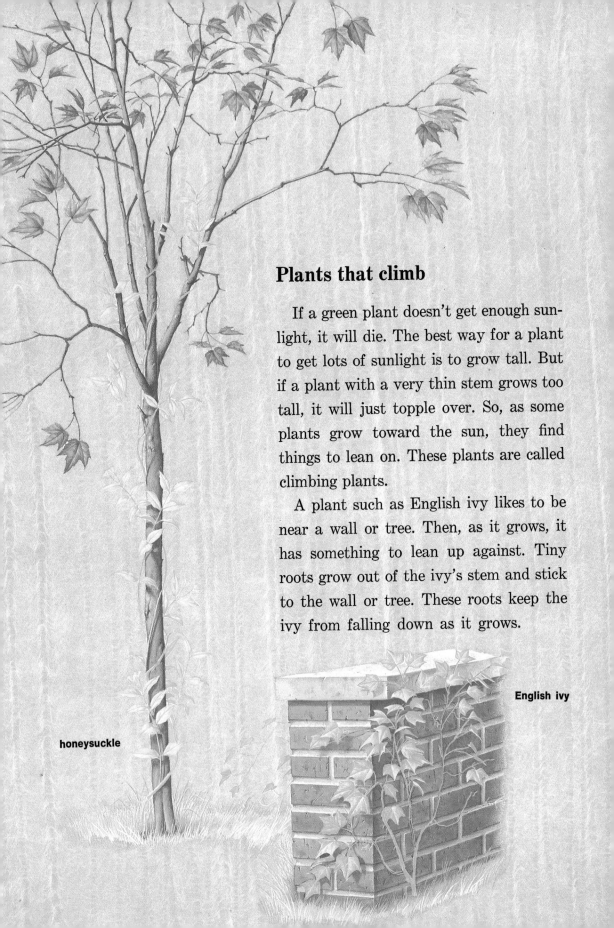

Plants that climb

If a green plant doesn't get enough sunlight, it will die. The best way for a plant to get lots of sunlight is to grow tall. But if a plant with a very thin stem grows too tall, it will just topple over. So, as some plants grow toward the sun, they find things to lean on. These plants are called climbing plants.

A plant such as English ivy likes to be near a wall or tree. Then, as it grows, it has something to lean up against. Tiny roots grow out of the ivy's stem and stick to the wall or tree. These roots keep the ivy from falling down as it grows.

English ivy

honeysuckle

Some plants wrap themselves around trees or other plants to keep from falling over. This is how honeysuckle grows.

Some plants send out leafy arms called tendrils. These tendrils wrap themselves around fence posts and other things. In this way, the plant keeps from falling over as it grows.

Every climbing plant has to have something to lean on when it starts to grow. If there is nothing for the climbing plant to hold on to, it begins to spread out on the ground. But if it doesn't get enough sunlight, it will die.

poison ivy

grapevine

Vampire plants

Some plants live like vampires.

They fasten themselves to other plants and suck food and water out of them!

When a plant called a dodder sprouts from the ground, it stretches out toward the nearest plant. The dodder's stem grows toward the other plant and slowly winds around it. The dodder pushes little threadlike roots into the other plant's stem. With these threads the dodder sucks food and water out of the other plant.

Finally, the dodder breaks loose from its own root. It spends the rest of its life wrapped around the other plant.

Mistletoe is a vampire plant, too. Mistletoe seeds are dropped on tree trunks by birds. The seeds send roots into the tree trunk. Then the mistletoe plant grows on the tree. The mistletoe can make some of its own food, but it gets all its water by sucking it out of the tree.

mistletoe

apple tree

Mistletoe is a vampire plant.
It often grows on apple trees.

When a young dodder sprouts,
it begins to grow toward
the nearest plant.

The dodder wraps itself around
the other plant. It gets its
food and water by sucking them
out of the other plant.

Indian paintbrush is a plant that seems to be minding its own business. But it's a vampire, too. Its roots spread through the ground and fasten to all the roots of other plants they can find. Then the Indian paintbrush sucks water and some food out of the roots of all its neighbors!

Plants that live on other plants are called parasites.

baobab "jail" tree

Odd and unusual trees

traveler's palm

The world is full of unusual trees.

One tree has fruits that look like big sausages hanging from its branches.

Another tree looks a little like a giant umbrella.

Still another tree looks somewhat like a peacock's tail.

And, in Australia, a large tree with a hollow trunk was once used as a jail.

"dropsical" tree

sausage tree

rain tree

The biggest living things

The blue whale is the largest animal that has ever lived—bigger than an elephant, bigger than the biggest dinosaur. But even the blue whale isn't the largest living thing on earth. Trees are. And the largest of all trees are the redwoods and giant sequoias that grow in California.

The tallest trees in the world are the California redwoods. Most of them are more than 300 feet (90 meters) high—about as tall as a 30-story building. The tallest known redwood is almost 370 feet (113 meters) high!

The giant sequoias are not as tall as the redwoods, but their trunks are much thicker. One big sequoia is called the General Sherman, after a famous soldier. The tree is 272 feet (83 meters) high. The widest part of its trunk is more than 100 feet (30 meters) around and more than 36 feet (11 meters) across. A big crowd of people could hide behind this tree!

redwood trees

sequoia trees ▶

The oldest living tree

If trees had birthday parties, there's one tree in the United States that would need more than 4,000 candles on its birthday cake!

Trees live much longer than people or animals do. A big oak tree, with a trunk so thick that you can't get your arms around it, may be hundreds of years old. The big redwood trees in California are thousands of years old.

The oldest known tree in the United States lives in a mountain forest in California. It's a gnarled, twisted bristlecone pine tree that's more than 4,600 years old. It is one of the oldest living things in the world.

bristlecone pine

cushion plant

The cushion plant

In New Zealand, there grows a plant that looks like a cushion made of white sheep's wool. It's called a cushion plant. And sometimes it's called a vegetable sheep.

A cushion plant is made up of thousands of tiny stems with millions of little leaves. The leaves are covered with tiny hairs, and that's what gives the plant its woolly look. The stems grow together so closely that they look like one big white lump.

You could even sit on a cushion plant if you wished. But you would be surprised. It isn't a bit soft—it's as hard as a rock!

Weeds and Wild Flowers

Queen Anne's Lace in frilly white,
*   Dandelions gold,*
Stalwart, seedy plantain spears:
*   These are weeds I'm told.*

Though many folks may call them weeds
*   And weeds they well may be,*
I stand and stand to look at them.
*   They're beautiful to me!*

WEEDS
Leland B. Jacobs

The lion's tooth

Dandelions are good to eat!

For years, people in different parts of the world have eaten the young, spring leaves of dandelions. Some people boil them and eat them with salt and pepper. Some people use them in salads. These spring leaves are called dandelion greens.

The dandelion got its name in a funny way. The jagged edges of the dandelion's leaf look like a row of teeth. So, long ago, the people in France gave the plant the name *dent de lion*, which means lion's tooth. But to the people in England, *dent de lion* sounded like dandelion, and that's what they called this plant!

There was a pretty dandelion
  With lovely, fluffy hair,
That glistened in the sunshine
  And in the summer air.
But oh! this pretty dandelion
  Soon grew old and gray;
And, sad to tell! her charming hair
  Blew many miles away.

DANDELION
Author Unknown

A tall plant with tasty seeds

Sunflowers are big plants with thick, hairy stems and big, heart-shaped leaves. Sunflower blossoms are often as big as dinner plates, and sunflowers sometimes grow twice as tall as a tall man.

Sunflower seeds were an important food for many American Indian tribes. The Indians dried the seeds and ground them into powder. They used the powder to make bread and thicken soup. Sometimes they mixed powdered sunflower seeds with fat to make a sort of pudding.

Sunflowers grow wild in prairies and meadows, but there are sunflower farms in many parts of the world. Oil from sunflower seeds is used to make margarine, cooking oils, paint, and soap. And many people enjoy eating sunflower seeds.

Jack-in-the-pulpit

Jack-in-the-pulpit

It's easy to see how this little plant got its name. It looks like a little man in a pulpit, ready to give a sermon. It's called Jack-in-the-pulpit because "Jack" is another word for a man or boy, just as "Jill" means a girl.

Jack-in-the-pulpit is sometimes called Indian turnip. That's because Indians used to eat the root, which looks somewhat like a turnip. The Indians didn't eat the roots raw, though. The roots have poison in them. The Indians let the roots dry in the sun for a long time. That got rid of the poison.

Jack-in-the-pulpit has a relative that grows in England and other parts of Europe. It looks much like Jack-in-the-pulpit, but is called a cuckoopint.

Jack-in-the-Pulpit
  Is preaching today.
What do you think
  He is going to say?

I'm sure I know well
  The message he'll bring:
Be glad for a green world!
  Be glad it is spring!

JACK-IN-THE-PULPIT
Leland B. Jacobs

Arrowhead

If you were an Indian long ago, you might have gone wading to get some of your food.

Arrowhead is a plant with arrow-shaped leaves that grows in water near the edges of streams and ponds. When Indians saw these plants, they might take off their moccasins and wade into the water. They would pull the plants out of the mud with their toes. Then they would boil the roots and eat them.

Arrowhead roots taste bitter when eaten raw. But when they are boiled they taste a lot like potatoes. Maybe that's why arrowhead is also called duck potato.

Indians liked to eat arrowhead roots. They pulled the plants out of the mud with their toes.

arrowhead

calamus

The perfume plant

Do you think it would be fun to have leaves on the floor of your house instead of a rug?

Long ago, people in Europe and early settlers in America would gather leaves of the calamus plant. They dried the leaves in the sun. Then they covered the floors of their houses with the leaves. The leaves had a nice, sweet smell that made a house smell good.

If you live near a pond, a stream, or a marsh, you might try drying some calamus leaves. Look for calamus—it is also called sweet flag—in shallow water. You'll know it by its long, swordlike leaves.

Long ago, people often gathered calamus leaves to put on the floors of their houses.

milkweed

A plant that bandages itself

There are lots of things to know about the plant called milkweed.

Milkweed gets its name from the white juice, which looks like milk, that oozes out when the plant is cut. This rubbery juice dries in the sun and covers the cut like a bandage.

Without milkweed plants, there might not be any beautiful monarch butterflies. Milkweed is the only plant on which female monarch butterflies will lay their eggs. That's because milkweed is the only food that monarch butterfly caterpillars will eat.

Milkweed seeds grow inside fat, green pods. In the fall, the pods turn brown, dry up, and split open. When the wind blows, the seeds are lifted out of the pod a few at a time. They have long, silky tufts, like parachutes, that carry them through the air on the wind.

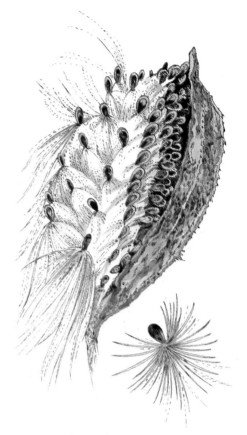

milkweed seeds in a pod

In a milkweed cradle,
Snug and warm,
Baby seeds are hiding,
Safe from harm.
Open wide the cradle,
Hold it high!
Come Mr. Wind,
Help them fly.

BABY SEEDS
Unknown

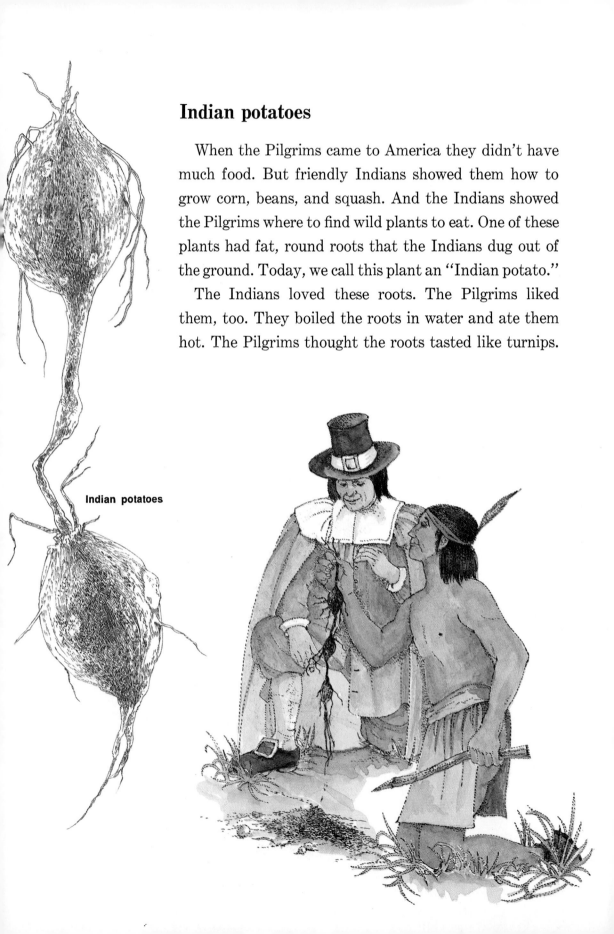

Indian potatoes

When the Pilgrims came to America they didn't have much food. But friendly Indians showed them how to grow corn, beans, and squash. And the Indians showed the Pilgrims where to find wild plants to eat. One of these plants had fat, round roots that the Indians dug out of the ground. Today, we call this plant an "Indian potato."

The Indians loved these roots. The Pilgrims liked them, too. They boiled the roots in water and ate them hot. The Pilgrims thought the roots tasted like turnips.

Indian potatoes

An Indian medicine plant

When you're sick, your mother or father calls a doctor.

Long ago, when Indian children became sick, their mothers or fathers called a medicine man. The medicine man didn't have pills or shots, but he could make many kinds of medicine from wild plants.

One plant the medicine man used was the May apple. With its slim stem and large green leaves, the May apple looks like a little umbrella. While it does bloom in May, its fruit doesn't appear until July or August, and looks more like a lemon than an apple.

The root of the May apple plant is actually poisonous and should never be eaten. But the medicine men boiled the roots in water. Then the water became a medicine that was good for curing a stomachache.

May apples

Elves' umbrellas and toads' stools

Fungi are strange little plants. They have no roots, stems, or leaves. They look like umbrellas, or balls, or sponges, or horns, or even birds' nests! They are white, or yellow, or orange, or purple, or even polka-dotted—but seldom green. They usually grow in damp, dark places in woods, in piles of rotting leaves, or on old trees and logs. And sometimes they pop up on peoples' lawns.

The fungi you probably know best are the ones called mushrooms. They usually look like little umbrellas. In fact, people once believed that elves used mushrooms for umbrellas when it rained.

Mushrooms are often called toadstools. Someone with a sense of humor must have made up that name. But some mushrooms are just about the right size and shape to make a comfortable stool for a fat toad.

Some mushrooms are good to eat. But some are poisonous and can kill! Many people believe that poisonous mushrooms will turn a spoon or a coin black, or will make water turn black, but that's not true. There's no way to tell a good mushroom from a poisonous one unless you're an expert. So never eat a wild mushroom!

fly agaric mushrooms

morel mushrooms

bird's nest fungi

puffballs

club mushrooms

Fairies, sneezes, and piles of gold

Long ago, people in Ireland believed that ragweed was the favorite plant of the fairies. But it seems strange that the fairies would like a plant that makes many people feel sick.

In most flowers there are tiny grains called pollen. Ragweed pollen is like dust. It floats in the air. When it gets into people's noses, it causes an allergy called hay fever. Hay fever makes some people's eyes itchy and red. It makes their noses run, too. But most of all, it makes them sneeze.

goldenrod

ragweed

The plant called goldenrod is often blamed for making people sneeze, too. But this is a mistake. Goldenrod pollen doesn't float in the air. It's heavy and sticky.

Goldenrod gets its name because it looks like a slim, green rod with a mass of gold at its tip. Its golden flowers bloom from late summer through autumn. They look like piles of gold along the sides of roads and in meadows.

The day's eye and a cup of butter

Did you ever wonder how some wild flowers got their names?

The daisy looks somewhat like an eye. And, like an eye, it opens up at the beginning of each day. So, long ago in England, people named it "day's eye." In time, the name became daisy.

The buttercup got its name because it looks like a cup made of yellow butter. Long ago, people believed that butter was yellow because cows ate buttercups. But that's not true. Butter does get its color from what cows eat, but cows don't eat buttercups.

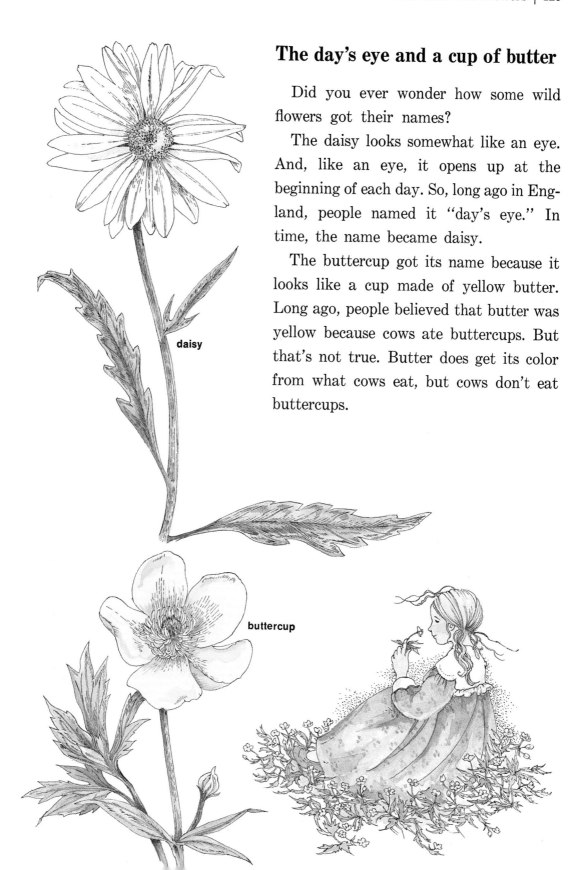

daisy

buttercup

cattails

"Cossack asparagus"

Cattails grow in marshes, on riverbanks, and near water-filled ditches. Their flowers become fuzzy, brown rods that look and feel like the tip of a cat's tail.

Cattail roots are good to eat. The Cossack people of Russia eat them, and so do many English people. In England they are called "Cossack asparagus."

A bunch of cattails was like a whole bagful of groceries for the Indians. The Indians ate cattail root bread, cattail flower soup, and boiled cattail stems.

People once found many uses for cattails. They dried the long leaves and wove them together to make seats for chairs. They stuffed mattresses with the soft, cottony down that comes from the brown rods. And they used cattails for decorations, as many people still do.

Pot-cleaning plants

When people clean pots and pans, they probably use scratchy pads of steel wool or plastic. But long ago, people cleaned pots with plants called horsetails.

Horsetails, also called rushes, are short, hollow-stemmed plants that grow in sandy places. They have a rough, sort of glassy covering on their stems. This is the same kind of stuff that makes sand scratchy. When the people of long ago scrubbed their pots with the scratchy horsetails, the pots got nice and shiny.

The word "scour" means to clean well. Because the horsetails did such a good cleaning job, people gave them the name "scouring rushes."

horsetails

The Indian lemonade plant

staghorn sumac

Sumac is a small tree or bush with narrow, pointed leaves. It tells people when fall arrives. Its leaves are usually the first to change color. They turn from green to a bright, glowing red.

Near the end of summer, bunches of red berries grow on some kinds of sumac trees. The American Indians made a drink from those berries. They dried the berries, mashed them, and mixed them with water. This made a sour, cooling drink that looked and tasted somewhat like pink lemonade.

One kind of sumac has white berries that hang down instead of sticking up as the red berries do. The Indians stayed away from that kind of sumac. It is poisonous and makes skin burn and itch!

The carrot's lacy cousin

From May until late August you can see the white, lacy flowers of a plant called Queen Anne's lace nodding at you along roads and in fields. The plant is named after a real queen who ruled England hundreds of years ago. People wore lots of lace on their clothes at that time, especially kings and queens. The person who named the flower probably thought it looked like the lace on the queen's dresses.

Queen Anne's lace is also called wild carrot because it is related to the kind of carrot we eat. But Queen Anne's lace isn't good to eat.

Queen Anne's lace

The plant that cats love

Many cats love the plant called catnip. A cat that finds a clump of catnip may happily roll about among the leaves. Many cat owners give their pets balls or toys made of dried catnip leaves. Most cats seem to like dried catnip leaves just as well as green, growing ones.

Some people like catnip, too—not to roll around in, but to drink. They make catnip tea by putting dried catnip leaves in boiling water and adding a little honey.

Catnip belongs to the mint family. It grows wild in many parts of North America and Europe. You can often find it along roads or near old farms.

When a cat finds a clump of catnip, it loves to roll over and over in the leaves.

catnip

A magic plant

Clover is a common plant. Its little red, white, pink, or yellow blossoms peep up from meadows and lawns everywhere.

Long ago, people believed that clover was a magic plant. They believed that three-leaf clovers would guard them from the spells of witches. They believed that four-leaf clovers would make them able to see fairies and elves. And, to this day, many people think that finding a four-leaf clover will bring them luck.

Of course clover isn't really a magic plant. But it does help make soil rich. And bees make fine honey from its blossoms.

clover

Deadly berries and seeds

Many kinds of berries and seeds are poisonous! People have died from eating mistletoe berries, yew berries, and castor beans. There are several kinds of nightshade plants with green, red, and black berries—all dangerous! Never eat a berry, seed, or nut unless you know for sure that it is safe.

yew berries

nightshade berries

castor beans
mistletoe berries

poison ivy

stinging nettle

Plants that make you itch and burn

The plants shown on this page can hurt you. If you should happen to touch one of them, it can make your skin burn and sting and itch. Learn to recognize these plants so you can stay away from them.

poison oak

Dangerous plants

Some of the most beautiful and common plants have leaves, petals, and branches that can kill! Never chew the leaves, flowers, or branches of any plant unless you are sure they are safe to eat.

oleander

The leaves and branches of the oleander are filled with poison.

rhubarb

We can eat the stems of the rhubarb plant. But its leaves will quickly bring death!

Cherries are good to eat. But the leaves and twigs of cherry trees contain a poison.

wild black cherry

mountain laurel

The leaves, twigs, and flowers
of the mountain laurel tree
can cause death.

The buds, fruits, and leaves
of the poinsettia plant
can cause illness.

poinsettia

How Does Your Garden Grow?

They can't see their pictures,
they can't read the label—
the seeds in a package—
so how are they able
to know if they're daisies
or greens for the table?

It sounds like a fancy,
it sounds like a fable,
but you do the sowing,
the weeding, the hoeing,
and they'll do the knowing
of how to be growing.

PACKAGE OF SEEDS
Aileen Fisher

A window-sill garden

You can have a bright, cheerful garden in your house all winter—a window-sill garden of house plants!

You can buy small house plants at many stores. Put them on a window sill, or on a table near a window where there is plenty of sunlight. Keep the dirt damp, but not muddy. Flower pots have holes in them to let water seep out, so put a dish under each pot to catch the water.

Some plants may grow bigger. If so, move them to bigger pots. You can use tin cans or cottage cheese cartons. Have your mother or father put a few small holes in the bottoms of these homemade pots.

Plants such as ivy or philodendron look nice in glass bowls. But a glass bowl must have gravel at the bottom to catch the water that seeps out of the dirt.

geranium   chives   ivy

a window-sill garden

Not all plants will grow indoors. Those that will are called house plants. They grow well if they get plenty of sunlight. The dirt should be kept damp, not muddy.

coleus   **cactus**

avocado

Living-room gardens

Would you like to have a garden in your living room? One way to do it is to buy house plants. Philodendrons, serpent's tongue, and rubber plants, which grow wild in hot parts of the world, make good house plants in cool places. These plants don't need much light—just a warm room, a little water, and a dusting now and then.

You can also sprout your own plants. You will need:

an avocado seed or	water
a sweet potato	potting soil
4 toothpicks	a planter
a jar	

Stick four toothpicks into opposite sides of an avocado seed. Place the seed,

serpent plant

sweet potato

philodendron

rubber plant

point up, in a jar partly filled with water. Rest the toothpicks on the rim of the jar, so that only the bottom of the seed is in water. Put the jar in a warm, light room. Soon the seed will sprout.

After the seed has sprouted roots and leaves, fill a planter with soil. Plant the seed in the center. Cover the roots and most of the seed with dirt, but don't cover the seed completely. Water your plant and place it in a warm sunny room. Now watch your garden grow! You can do this with a sweet potato, too.

Gardens in glass boxes

A terrarium is an indoor garden in a glass box. Owning one is like having a tiny forest, all to yourself.

You can buy a terrarium, but it's more fun to make your own. You'll need:

a glass box, bowl, or jar	a little sand
pebbles	peat moss
potting soil	water
	small plants

Put a layer of pebbles on the bottom for water to drain into. Cover the pebbles with potting soil, mixed with a little sand and peat moss. Water the soil until it is damp, but not muddy.

Next, dig up some ferns, moss, and other small plants from your yard or an empty lot. If you want, you can also buy small plants. Arrange the plants so that your terrarium looks like a tiny forest.

Keep your terrarium where it gets light, but not in a sunny place. If you cover your terrarium, the temperature and moisture should stay in balance. If the glass does get too moist, remove the lid for a short time.

You can raise water plants and fish in an aquarium. You will probably have to buy the plants and fish from a pet store. Many pet stores have books that tell you how to take care of the plants and fish and keep them healthy.

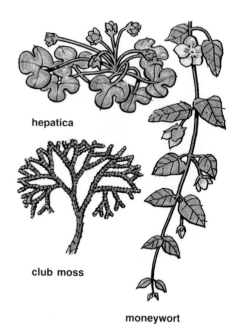

hepatica

club moss

moneywort

These are good plants to put into a terrarium.

These are some of the best plants for an aquarium.

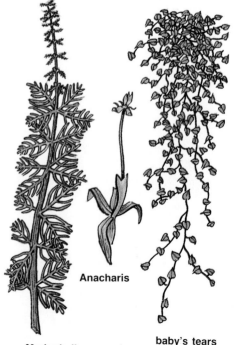

Anacharis

Myriophyllum

baby's tears

Outdoor gardens

A little seed
For me to sow . . .
A little earth
To make it grow . . .
A little hole,
A little pat . . .
A little wish,
And that is that.
A little sun,
A little shower . . .
A little while,
And then—a flower!

MAYTIME MAGIC
Mabel Watts

Planting an outdoor garden is truly fun! It's a thrill to watch little green heads come poking up from the places where you planted seeds!

All you need for an outdoor garden is a small patch of earth that gets plenty of sunshine. You can buy seeds for many kinds of outdoor plants. To plant them, just read the directions on the seed package.

The next few pages will show you some of the different kinds of outdoor gardens you might like to have.

a backyard garden

Wherever there's a little bit of
soil, there can be a garden. And a
garden brings beauty wherever it is.

rock garden

Rock gardens aren't very easy
to make. But they're fun, and
many people think they're the
most beautiful kind of garden.
Your rock garden won't have
to be as big as this one. But
it can be just as pretty if you
work hard at it.

A rock garden

If your yard has a sunny place that slopes a little, like a small hill, you can have a good rock garden. It should look like a tiny bit of mountainside where small, bright flowers grow among the rocks.

First, bring all your rocks to the slope. Put the biggest ones at the bottom. Scoop out shallow holes for them. At least half of each rock should be buried in the dirt.

Next, put the smaller stones higher up on the slope. Place some of them close together, but leave lots of dirt between others.

Finally, plant small ferns and flowering plants in the dirt between the rocks. Early spring is a good time to plant. Use plants that won't grow more than 12 inches (30 centimeters) high. Some good rock garden plants are shown on this page.

grape hyacinth

ostrich plume fern

sweet alyssum

hen and chickens

A vegetable garden

Nothing tastes quite so good as food you have grown yourself. To grow your own vegetables you will need a small bit of flat ground that gets *plenty* of sunshine.

It's easier to grow tomatoes from young plants than from seeds. Dig holes about two feet (60 centimeters) apart. Dig the holes deep enough to bury the roots and wide enough to let them spread out. Fill the holes with water and let it soak in. Rest the roots at the bottom of the hole. Cover them with dirt until the ground is level. Next to each plant put a stick about four feet (1.2 meters) high. As the plant grows, tie the stem to the stick.

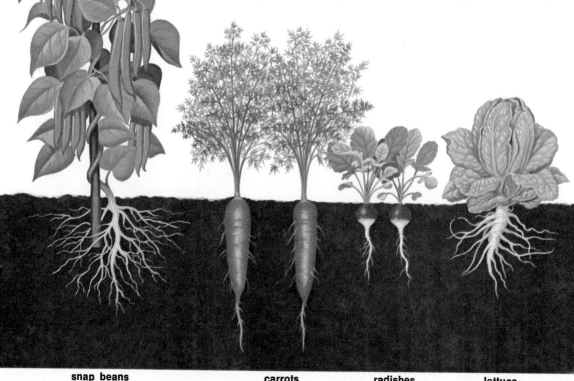

snap beans   **carrots**   **radishes**   **lettuce**

All the other vegetables shown on these pages—and many other vegetables—can be grown from seeds. Follow the directions on the packages. Water your vegetables only when there hasn't been much rain.

For more about the planning, planting, and care of a garden, look on pages 156–159.

On a summer vine, and low,
The fat tomatoes burst and grow;

A green, a pink, a yellow head,
Will soon be warm and shiny red;

And on a morning hot with sun,
I'll find and pick a ripened one.

Warm juice and seeds beneath the skin—
I'll shut my eyes when I bite in.

TOMATO TIME
Myra Cohn Livingston

cucumbers   **tomatoes**

Flowers you plant every spring

Most flowers that you plant in the spring are annuals. Annuals are plants that live only one summer. They sprout from seeds that are planted in the spring. In the summer, their flowers grow and make seeds. In the fall, the plants die. You must save their seeds, or buy new seeds, to plant again in the spring.

The plants shown on these two pages are annuals. Most of them grow from seeds. You can buy packages of flower seeds at many stores. But be sure you read the

gladiolus   red salvia   marigold

instructions on the package before planting the seeds. In different parts of the world, spring comes at different times. The package will tell you when and how deep to plant the seeds.

Gladiolus plants are not really annuals, but where winters are cold we treat them like annuals. The plants grow from underground buds called corms. The corms are planted in the spring. In autumn, they are dug up and stored. Next spring, they are planted again.

For more about the planning, planting, and care of a garden, look on pages 156-159.

zinnias   snapdragon   sweet peas

Flowers you plant only once

Some flowers don't have to be planted every year. You plant them just once, and leave them in the ground. From then on they bloom each spring.

Plants that bloom every year are called perennials. The plants shown on these two pages are some favorite perennials.

Lilies, tulips, crocuses, and irises grow from underground buds called bulbs or corms. You can buy bulbs at many stores. Most bulbs should be planted in the fall. But the package the bulbs come in will tell

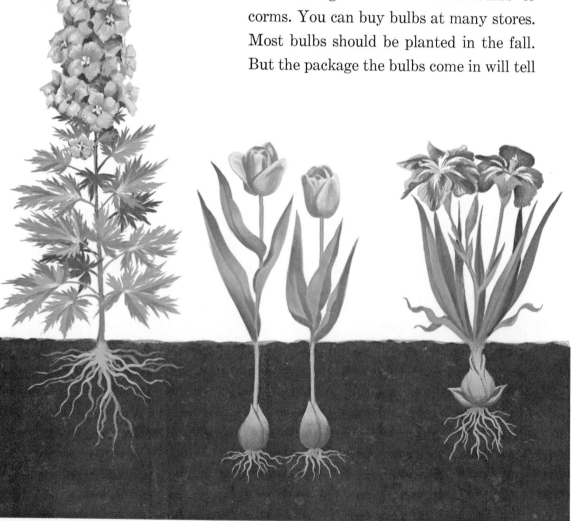

delphinium   tulips   iris

you the best time to plant them. And remember, plant bulbs with their pointed ends sticking up.

Delphiniums and chrysanthemums grow from seeds, or from seedlings, which are small plants that are already growing. They should be planted in the spring.

Many perennials need protection during winter. The package your seeds or bulbs come in, or a gardening book will tell you what to do for each kind.

For more about the planning, planting, and care of a garden, look on pages 156-159.

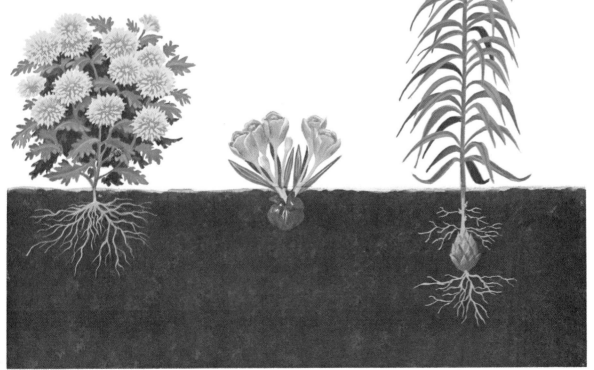

chrysanthemum   crocus   lily

A fun garden

All the plants shown on these two pages are "fun" plants. They have bright colors and unusual shapes. Several of them can be saved and used to decorate your house during winter or for special occasions.

Honesty and strawflowers are planted in early spring. Honesty blooms in May and June. The flowers become silvery seed pods that can be dried and put in a vase. Strawflowers bloom from midsummer until the first frost. They can be cut, dried, and used for decorations, too.

Gourds should also be planted in early spring. They ripen in the fall, growing into many shapes and sizes, with stripes and bright patterns. They will keep for years, and can be varnished or painted. Both gourds and Indian corn are often used as decorations for Halloween parties and Thanksgiving Day feasts.

flowering kale

Indian corn

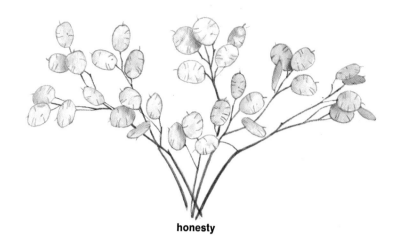

honesty

bells of Ireland

Chinese lanterns

gourds

strawflowers

Gardening tips

Before you can start your garden, you must pick a good place for it. Most garden plants need lots of sunshine, so choose a place the sun shines on most of the day.

Next, dig up the ground, turn it over, and rake it smooth. Your mother or father may have to help you do this.

When the ground is ready, mark off rows for the seeds or plants you're going to put in. Pound sturdy, pointed sticks into the ground. Then stretch twine between them as the children have done in the picture on the opposite page.

To make holes for seeds, push a pointed stick into the ground. If you're going to put in baby plants that are already growing, such as onions or tomatoes, you'll need a trowel. Use it like a big spoon, to scoop out holes.

To loosen soil, or dig up weeds, you can use a hand cultivator. Kneel down and pull it over the ground like a little rake.

Water the earth around each baby plant or seed until it is damp but not muddy.

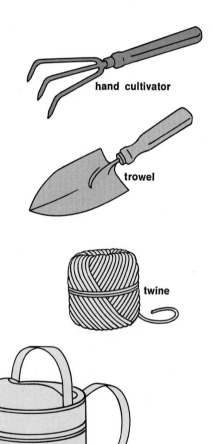

hand cultivator

trowel

twine

watering can

Spring Planting

This is how your garden might look when you start your spring planting. Each row of plants or seeds is marked off with string. The empty seed packages show what has been planted in each row. Most of the plants have been put where they will get plenty of sunshine. Many—but not all—growing plants need lots of sunshine. Some, like pansies, do well, or even better, in the shade. So these children have planted their pansies in the shade of the tree.

(Turn to next page)

Summer Weeding

By early summer, garden plants are usually well up—but so are the weeds! Here, the girl is pulling up weeds by hand, while the boy is using a hoe. He is looking at an insect that was eating one of his potato plants. He'll have to find a way to protect these plants from insects. The children will also have to water their garden if there is not much rain. If you have to water your garden, do it after the sun goes down. Then the sun won't dry up the water before it soaks in.

Autumn Harvesting

When it's time to harvest, the garden rewards you for all your hard work. Your flowers can be harvested as soon as they bloom. Picking garden flowers will help more to bloom. It's not so easy to tell when to pull up vegetables that grow in the ground. But the pictures on pages 148-149 will show you what some of these plants look like when they are ready for harvesting. And if you've planted any pumpkins, they'll be big and orange just in time for Halloween.

Famous Gardens

Many people have small gardens in their yards, on a porch or patio, or even in a sunny window.

But people have also made big gardens. Some are parks that go on for miles. Some are indoors, in buildings made just for them.

These big gardens are useful. They often have plants from many parts of the world. So, scientists can study these plants without traveling to distant places. And people can see plants they might never see otherwise.

Even more important, these gardens are beautiful. They are a pleasure to see and walk in. People from all over the world come to visit them.

Indoor gardens

We usually think of gardens as being outdoor places. But many beautiful gardens are indoors, in special buildings. The plants get plenty of sunlight through glass roofs, and are kept warm all year long. So, even if there is snow on the ground outside, an indoor garden is always green and flowering.

Botanical Garden, Munich, Germany

Duke Gardens, Somerville, New Jersey

Longwood Gardens, Kennett Square, Pennsylvania

Chateau Garden, Villandry, France

Formal gardens

A formal garden is planted in careful designs. The flowers are arranged in squares, circles, or fancy shapes. Bushes are often trimmed to points, squares, or balls. Paths are long and straight.

Hampton Court Garden,
Middlesex, England

Royal Gardens,
Hannover, Germany

Natural gardens

Natural gardens are often called wild gardens because they look just like an ordinary woodland or meadow. But most of the plants in a natural garden are carefully planted by people.

A natural garden may be small or it may be big enough to have lakes or streams or mountains in it.

National Botanic Garden, Kirstenbosch, South Africa

azaleas in full bloom
at Magnolia Gardens,
Charleston,
South Carolina

Strybing Arboretum,
San Francisco, California

Favorite gardens

In every part of the world, people have a favorite kind of garden.

In Japan, people like gardens that have little bridges in them. In India, gardens often have ponds filled with water lilies. Gardens in Hawaii may have many ferns.

Gardeners in other parts of the world often copy these favorite gardens.

Foster Botanic Garden, Honolulu, Hawaii

**Daigo Temple Garden,
Kyoto, Japan**

**Botanic Garden,
Calcutta, India**

Mount Usher Garden, Ashford, Ireland

Meet the Trees

Can you tell an oak tree from a maple tree? Can you tell one kind of Christmas tree from another?

There are many different kinds of trees. But each kind of tree has leaves, bark, fruit, flowers, and seeds that are different from those of every other kind of tree.

On the next 15 pages is a game about trees. Can you find your way through a spooky forest? If you take the wrong path, you'll be in danger. But if you learn to tell one kind of tree from another, you'll always be on the right path.

So, come on—meet the trees!

The tree-path game

Come take a walk through this spooky forest. But be careful! If you choose a wrong path you'll be captured by giant spiders or eaten by crocodiles!

You can play this game by yourself. It begins here and ends on page 186. On all the game pages you'll find pictures of the forest, with many paths. You must take the right paths to get "home."

Each picture has a signboard that tells you what paths to take. Each path is marked by a picture of a leaf, or bark, or some other part of a tree. So, if the signboard says to take the "oak path," you must look for the path that has something from an oak tree next to it.

If you don't know much about trees, look at the tree identification chart below the picture. If you need to find an oak path, look for the oak tree on the chart. Under the oak tree are pictures of an oak tree's leaf, nut, flower, and bark. Look for the path that has a picture of one of these things next to it. It's the oak path.

If you take a wrong path, you'll know it when you turn the page. All wrong paths lead into danger. When you find you have taken a wrong path, turn back and try to find the right one.

TAKE THE APPLE PATH, THEN TAKE THE BASSWOOD PATH

Use this tree identification chart to find the right paths.

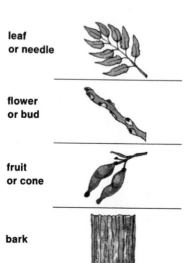

ailanthus

leaf or needle

flower or bud

fruit or cone

bark

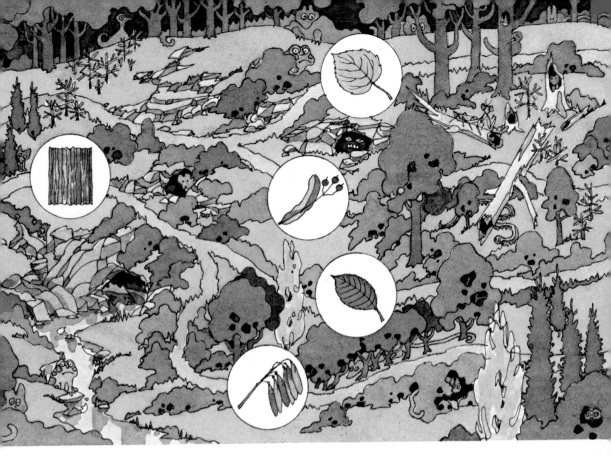

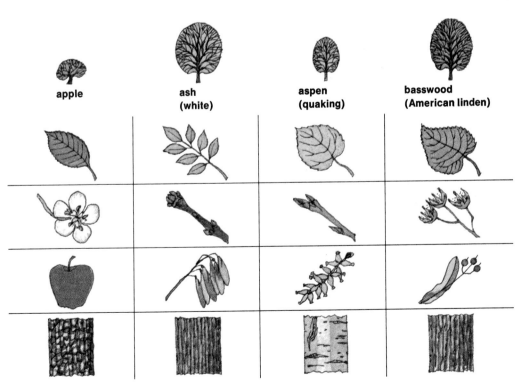

apple	ash (white)	aspen (quaking)	basswood (American linden)

173

Did you take the wrong path? Look at these clues to find your mistake.

 apple

 basswood

 apple

 ailanthus

 ash

 aspen

Use this tree identification chart to find the right paths. Start the game on page 172.

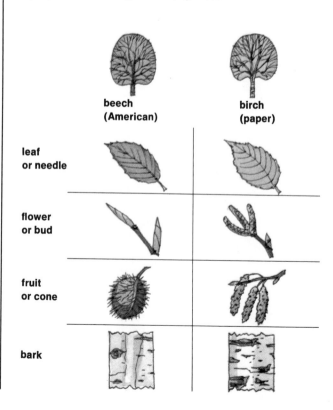

	beech (American)	birch (paper)
leaf or needle		
flower or bud		
fruit or cone		
bark		

174

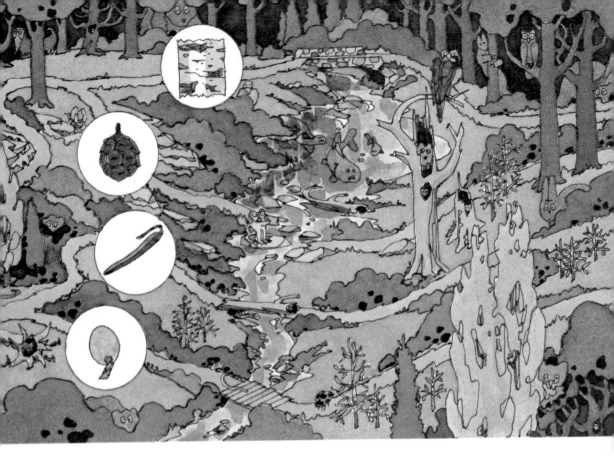

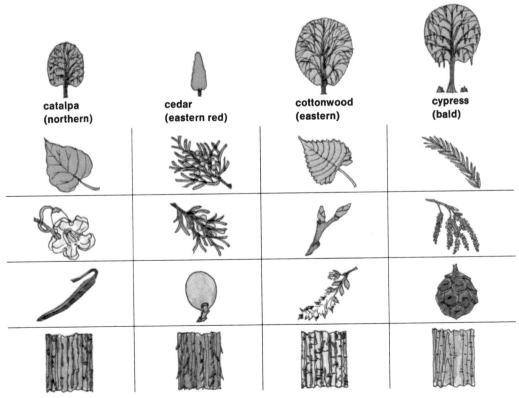

catalpa (northern)	cedar (eastern red)	cottonwood (eastern)	cypress (bald)

Did you take the wrong path? Look at these clues to find your mistake.

 cottonwood

 catalpa

 birch

 beech

 cypress

 cedar

Use this tree identification chart to find the right paths. Start the game on page 172.

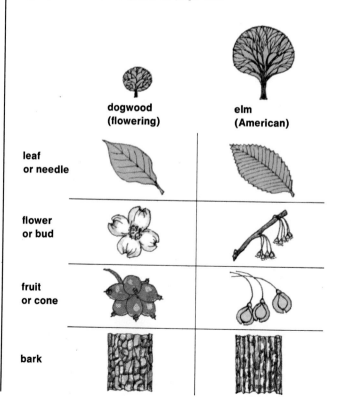

	dogwood (flowering)	elm (American)
leaf or needle		
flower or bud		
fruit or cone		
bark		

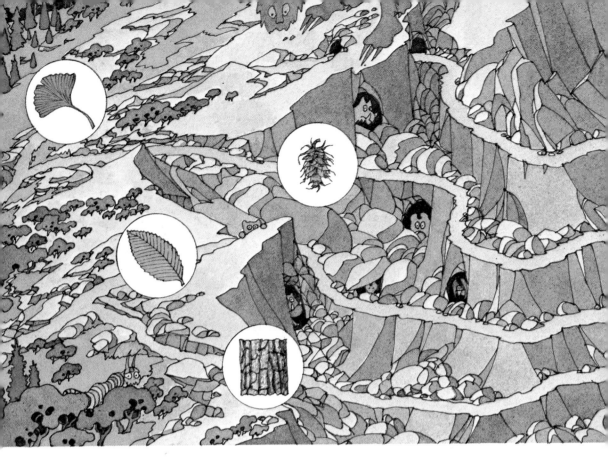

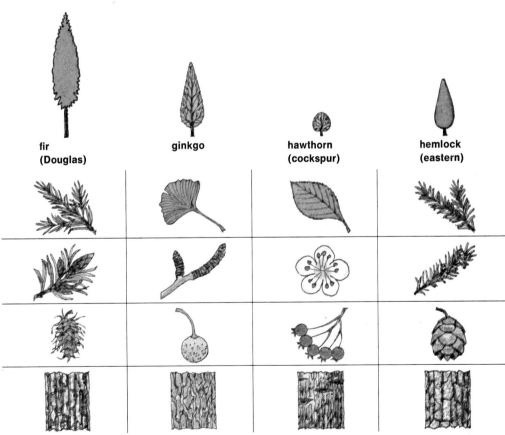

fir (Douglas)	ginkgo	hawthorn (cockspur)	hemlock (eastern)

Did you take the wrong path? Look at these clues to find your mistake.

 dogwood

 ginkgo

 fir

 elm

 hemlock

 hawthorn

Use this tree identification chart to find the right paths. Start the game on page 172.

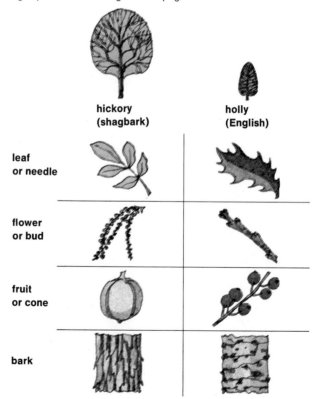

	hickory (shagbark)	holly (English)
leaf or needle		
flower or bud		
fruit or cone		
bark		

178

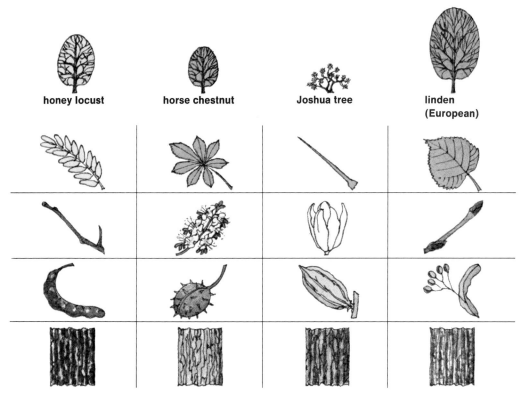

honey locust	horse chestnut	Joshua tree	linden (European)

Did you take the wrong path? Look at these clues to find your mistake.

 hickory

 Joshua tree

 horse chestnut

 holly

 honey locust

 linden

Use this tree identification chart to find the right paths. Start the game on page 172.

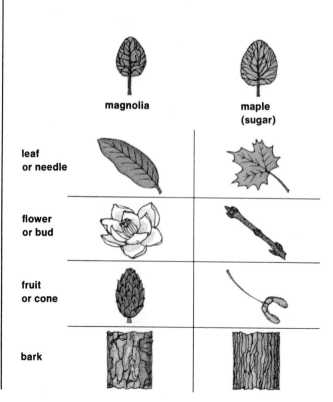

	magnolia	maple (sugar)
leaf or needle		
flower or bud		
fruit or cone		
bark		

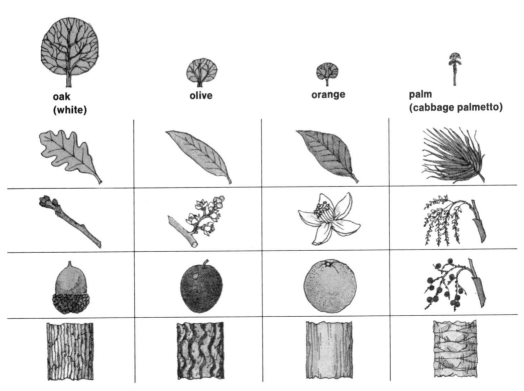

oak (white)	olive	orange	palm (cabbage palmetto)

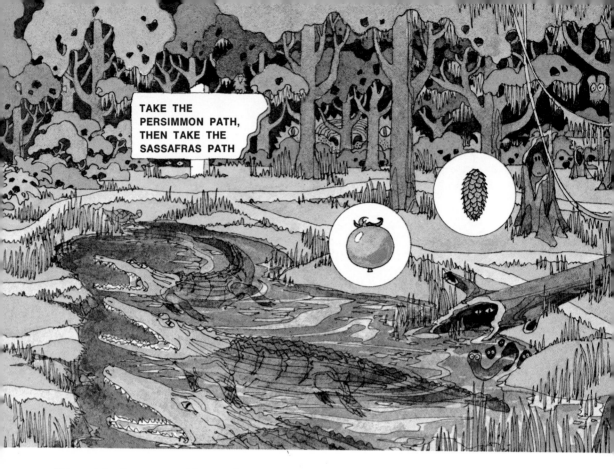

Did you take the wrong path? Look at these clues to find your mistake.

 magnolia

 olive

 oak

 orange

 palm

 maple

Use this tree identification chart to find the right paths. Start the game on page 172.

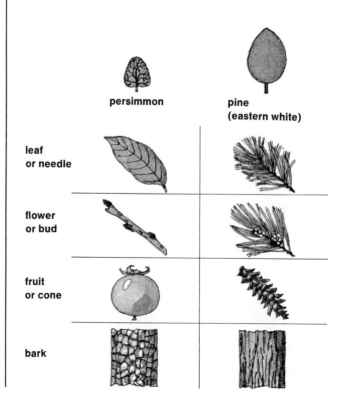

	persimmon	pine (eastern white)
leaf or needle		
flower or bud		
fruit or cone		
bark		

182

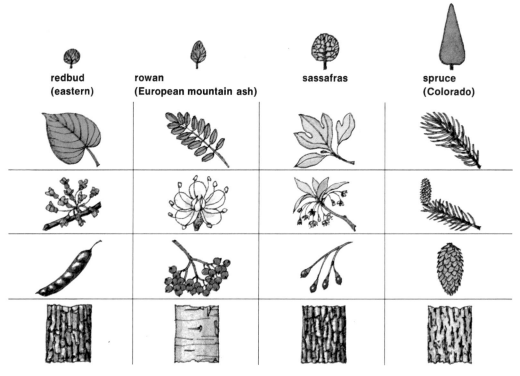

redbud (eastern)	rowan (European mountain ash)	sassafras	spruce (Colorado)

TAKE THE SWEET GUM PATH, THEN TAKE THE WILLOW PATH

Did you take the wrong path? Look at these clues to find your mistake.

 persimmon

 spruce

 sassafras

 pine

 rowan

 redbud

Use this tree identification chart to find the right paths. Start the game on page 172.

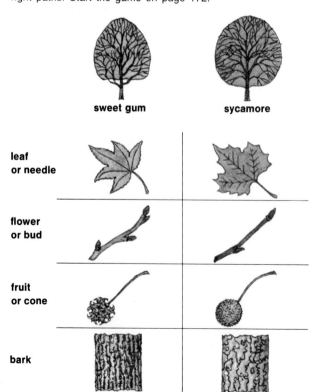

	sweet gum	sycamore
leaf or needle		
flower or bud		
fruit or cone		
bark		

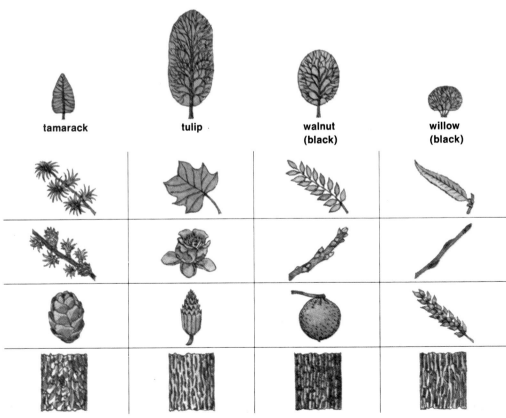

tamarack	tulip	walnut (black)	willow (black)

YOU'VE WON!
TAKE THE
RAINBOW ROAD
TO HOME

Did you take the wrong path? Look at these clues
to find your mistake. Start the game on page 172.

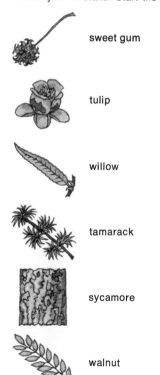

sweet gum

tulip

willow

tamarack

sycamore

walnut

Solving tree mysteries

How would you like to be a tree detective? To be a tree detective you have to be able to use clues to find out the names of the trees you see.

You can use the tree charts on pages 172-185 to help you in your detective work. These charts show more than 40 common trees. Under each tree's name and picture, the parts of the tree are shown—its leaf or needle, its flower or bud, its fruit or cone, and its bark.

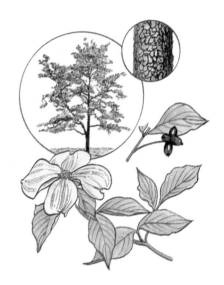

flowering dogwood

Take this book with you when you start your detective work. There are probably several kinds of trees growing near your house. Look first at a tree's leaves. They're your first clue. Compare a leaf with the leaves shown in the identification chart. If you can find a picture that looks just like your real leaf, you're getting warm.

Next, look at the bark on your tree. Does it look like the picture of the bark that's under the leaf picture? If it doesn't, you're barking up the wrong tree. Keep looking at the chart. Can you find a tree that has a leaf, bark, and other things that look just like those on the real tree? If you can, you've solved the mystery. You've learned the tree's name.

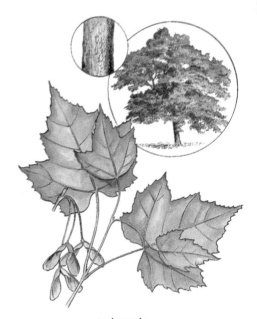

red maple

Leaf-scar faces

Some trees have "faces"! You can see them in the fall, if you look closely.

When leaves drop off a tree, scars are left. The scars often look like the faces of animals—or even creatures from another planet. They appear where new leaves will grow, so they are called leaf-scar faces.

Different trees have different leaf-scar faces. Four kinds are shown on these pages. What do you think they look like?

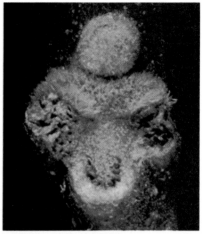

butternut leaf-scar face

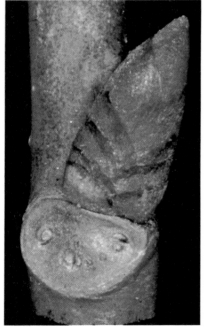

elm leaf-scar face

ash leaf-scar face

◀ **poplar leaf-scar face**

Christmas tree favorites

Which is your favorite kind of Christmas tree?

People in the United States and Canada usually choose the balsam fir, the black spruce, or the Douglas fir. People in Britain, Germany, and most of Europe like the silver fir and the Norway spruce. And the hardy Scots (or Scotch) pine is becoming a favorite with many people in both North America and Europe.

You can tell these trees by their shapes, by their needles, and by their cones.

balsam fir

silver fir

Douglas fir

Norway spruce

Scots (Scotch) pine

black spruce

Plants of Long Ago

The plants that grew on earth hundreds of millions of years ago didn't look much like the plants we see around us today.

Scientists have learned a great deal about what the world was like long ago. The men and women who study these things have put facts and ideas together. They have given us a story of how they think the world has changed in the course of billions of years. According to them, we owe a lot to the strange-looking plants of long ago.

Here, then, is part of the story that these scientists have worked out.

Long ago, the land was empty. All the plants and animals lived in the water. They looked like tiny blobs of jelly.

The first plants

Many hundreds of millions of years ago, the world was a scary place! Fiery volcanoes boomed and rumbled. The sky was filled with black ash. There was nothing but huge, gray ocean and bare, rocky land. There was no living thing *anywhere* on the land—not one plant or animal of any kind!

But in the seas there were millions of living creatures. They were so tiny you couldn't have seen them without a microscope. They looked like drops of jelly filled with bubbles.

Many of these tiny creatures were green. They were plants—the first plants in the world.

The air makers

Most scientists think that the first tiny sea plants made it possible for life to come onto the land.

To live, plants and animals must take in a gas called oxygen. The tiny sea plants and animals of billions of years ago got oxygen from the water, just as fish and sea plants do today. But scientists think that long ago there was no oxygen in the world's air. So there were no land plants or animals because there was no way for them to get oxygen.

When plants make their food—out of sunlight, water, and carbon dioxide gas—they give off oxygen. The tiny sea plants of long ago gave off tiny bubbles of oxygen. The bubbles rose to the top of the water and burst. Tiny puffs of oxygen went into the air.

For millions and millions of years, billions and billions of tiny plants put oxygen into the air. Finally, there was enough oxygen in the air so that plants and animals could live on the land.

Scientists think that the first oxygen in the air came from tiny sea plants.

The plants that conquered the land

Scientists think that the first living thing on land came out of the water about 500 million years ago.

The sea was full of living things. There were jellyfish, sponges, worms, and small, crablike animals called trilobites. And there were plants growing in the shallow water near the shore.

Slowly, as many years passed, the plants grew toward the shore. At last they were growing right out of the water, creeping onto the land. They didn't look like much—probably like bunches of flat leaves or stubby green stems. But they were the first things in the world to live on the land.

Plants that came out of the water were the first living things on land. These plants helped to make the first soil.

The soil makers

Hundreds of millions of years ago, all the land was just bare, hard rock, sand, or clay. Now, soil covers most of the land. Where did the soil come from?

Plants and weather made it. The first living things on land were plants that grew out of water onto wet rocks. The plants pushed tiny roots into cracks in the rocks. Slowly, with the help of wind and rain, the roots broke the rocks and crumbled them into tiny pieces.

As plants died, they too broke into tiny pieces. And this mixture of crumbled rock and dead plants lying on the wet rocks was the first soil.

The first plants to live on land helped make the first soil in which other plants could live and grow. And every plant that has lived and died since, has helped make more of the soil that now covers most of the land.

The snaky plants

About 400 million years ago, the plants on land looked like snakes with stalks on their backs.

The long, snaky, rootlike stems of these plants curled over the ground. Tiny hairs grew out of the stems and reached into the ground to find water. Scaly stalks without leaves or flowers grew up out of the stems. The stalks were about three feet (1 meter) high.

There were no trees or grass or flowers anywhere. Just the strange, snaky plants, growing on the shores of lakes and quiet pools of water.

Use this small picture to find out the names of the plants in the big picture.

whisk fern

This plant looks very much like some of the plants that lived 400 million years ago.

Today, horsetails are small.
But millions of years ago,
they were as tall as trees.

horsetails

Psaronius ▶

Sigillaria ▶

▲
Lepidodendron

▲
Calamites

◀ Sphenophylum

The forests that turned to coal

The air was hot and wet. The ground was soft and oozy. Dragonflies with wings as long as your arm hummed through the air. Cockroaches as big as your fist hurried about. And, growing thickly everywhere, were strange towering trees and other plants.

That's what a forest was like during the Coal Age, 300 million years ago.

We call it the Coal Age because the trees and plants that grew then became the coal we use today. The plants in these forests grew and died and fell down. They were quickly covered by other plants that died and fell. All these dead plants were squeezed together. Slowly, during millions of years, they became the coal some people burn for heat.

Some of the trees in the coal forests looked like Christmas trees. Others were not like trees at all—they were strange, giant plants. One of them was an ancient relative of the plant called a horsetail, which grows near lakes and ponds. Today horsetails are only about 3 feet (1 meter) tall. But in the coal forests, they were more than 50 feet (15 meters) tall.

Use this small picture
to find out the names of the
plants in the big picture.

fossil of a 30-million-year-old plant

Looking at plants of long ago

How would you like to see a *real* leaf that might have been touched by a dinosaur—a leaf that's more than 100 million years old? It seems almost impossible, but such leaves really have been found!

Leaves of long-ago plants fell to the ground, just as leaves do today. Sometimes the leaves fell into streams and rivers. The water carried them along and finally buried them in mudbanks.

After many years the streams dried up. The mudbanks hardened into rock. And the leaves were pressed tight inside the rock. But by soaking the rock with acid, and splitting it, we can see the leaves— leaves that still have the same shape they had millions of years ago!

fossil of a 300-million-year-old plant

Sometimes leaves and other parts of long-ago plants left prints in the mud, just as you can make a print by pressing something into clay. When the mud hardened into rock, the prints were still there. And sometimes leaves, flowers, and even tree trunks were turned into coal or stone.

All these leaves, and prints, and parts of plants that have changed to stone and coal are called fossils. And it is from these fossils that we know what the plants of long ago were like.

fossil of a 300-million-year-old plant

fossil ferns and a lump of coal

What Plants Do for Us

Plants do a lot for us. We couldn't live without them.

Plants give us vegetables, fruits, cereals, and most other foods we eat.

Plants give us wood for building houses and making furniture.

Plants give us cotton, linen, and other kinds of cloth for clothes, towels, sheets, and other things we use.

Plants give us paper, rubber, string, and medicines. They even give us the fresh air we breathe!

And—just as important—plants give us pleasure. For, what sort of a world would it be if there were no shady trees, green grass, or lovely flowers?

Fresh air to breathe

Did you know that every green plant in the world is like a kind of factory? It works from sunrise to sunset making food for itself. As it produces food, it gives off an invisible gas called oxygen. The oxygen from plants mixes with other invisible gases that make up the air.

Oxygen is a very important gas! People, and all other animals, must have oxygen to live. When we breathe, our bodies take in the oxygen we need. Without oxygen in the air, we would die.

People and other animals that live on land take oxygen out of the air when they breathe. You might think that all the oxygen would soon be used up. It would be, if it weren't for the green plants! All day long, they keep releasing oxygen into the air.

You can watch a plant make oxygen. You will need:

- an Elodea plant (waterweed)
- a wide jar
- water
- a funnel (a clear one if possible)
- a clear plastic tube or bottle
- your kitchen sink

Lay the jar, funnel, and tube or bottle on their sides in the sink. Run cool water in the sink deep enough to cover them and fill them completely.

Put the Elodea plant in the jar. Next, slide the wide end of the funnel into the jar and over the plant. Then slide the plastic tube or bottle over the funnel. Stand the jar upright with the plant, funnel, and tube in it, as shown.

After a while, you will see a few bubbles begin to rise through the funnel. As the plant makes oxygen, the bubbles will move up through the water. Soon the top of the tube will be filled with oxygen the Elodea plant gives off as it makes food for itself.

An Elodea plant making oxygen

The funnel is over the Elodea plant, and the test tube is over the funnel. The bubble is oxygen just made by the plant. Because oxygen is a gas, the bubble is rising through the water.

After a while, the top of the test tube is filled with oxygen made by the Elodea plant.

Seeds, stems, and salad stuff

All the foods we call vegetables come from some part of a plant.

Lima beans, peas, and kidney beans are plant seeds.

Radishes, carrots, and beets are plant roots.

Onions are plant bulbs. Potatoes are the underground stems of a plant.

Celery and rhubarb are the stalks of plants.

Broccoli and cauliflower are the flowers, buds, and stems of plants. Cabbage is the bud of a plant.

Lettuce is the leaves of a plant.

And when we eat string beans or scarlet runner beans, we're eating seed pods, which are the fruits of plants.

Seeds and Seed Pods

peas   Lima beans   scarlet runner beans   kidney beans

Roots, Bulbs, and Underground Stems   **Flowers, Buds, Stems, and Leaves**

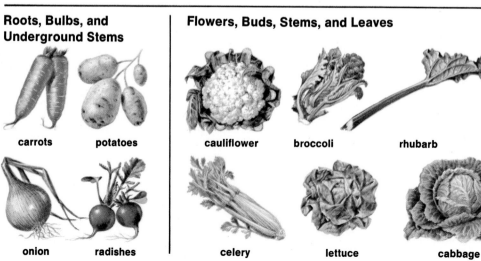

carrots   potatoes   cauliflower   broccoli   rhubarb

onion   radishes   celery   lettuce   cabbage

Sweet and tasty seed packages

Anything that grows on a plant and has seeds inside it is a fruit. A fruit is really just a package with one or more plant seeds in it.

Many kinds of fruits are good to eat. Apples, oranges, pears, peaches, plums, and dates are sweet seed packages that come from trees. Blueberries, gooseberries, strawberries, raspberries, and huckleberries are the seed packages of shrubs. Grapes, cranberries, and watermelons are the seed packages of vines.

Cucumbers, squash, pumpkins, and tomatoes are tasty packages of seeds, too. Even though we call them vegetables, they are really fruits!

Fruits

apple   orange   peach   date

blackberry   grapes   watermelon

Fruits We Call Vegetables

cucumber   pumpkin   tomato

Bread, breakfast food, and popcorn

Do you know that you probably eat grass?

When we think of grass we usually think of green lawns. But there are many kinds of grass. Wheat, oats, rye, barley, rice, and corn (which is called maize in many parts of the world) are all grasses. These grasses are called cereals. And their fruits, which we eat, are called grains.

Grains are one of the most important foods we get from plants. Without grains we wouldn't have bread, cookies, breakfast cereals, rice for chop suey—or popcorn to munch on at the movies!

Sugar, syrup, and spices

Most sugar comes from different parts of two plants. Some sugar comes from the long, white root of the sugar-beet plant. Some sugar comes from the juicy stem of the sugar-cane plant, which is a kind of grass.

All syrup and honey come from plants. Maple syrup is the sap of the sugar maple tree. Molasses is made from sugar-cane juice. Honey is made by bees from the nectar of many kinds of flowers.

Nearly all the spices that make your tongue tingle come from plants, too. Pepper is the dried, ground-up berries of a shrub. Cinnamon is the bark of a tree. Mustard, which goes so well on a hot dog, is made from the ground-up seeds of a small plant with yellow flowers. And most other spices are the dried leaves, stems, flowers, or seeds of little plants called herbs.

harvesting wheat

Sugar, syrup, and honey
all come from plants.
So do pepper, mustard,
and most other spices.

sugar
beet

sugar
cane

mustard

black
pepper

cutting sugar cane

Bread, breakfast food,
and popcorn are all made
from the fruit of plants
called cereals.

rice

wheat

oats

barley

rye

corn

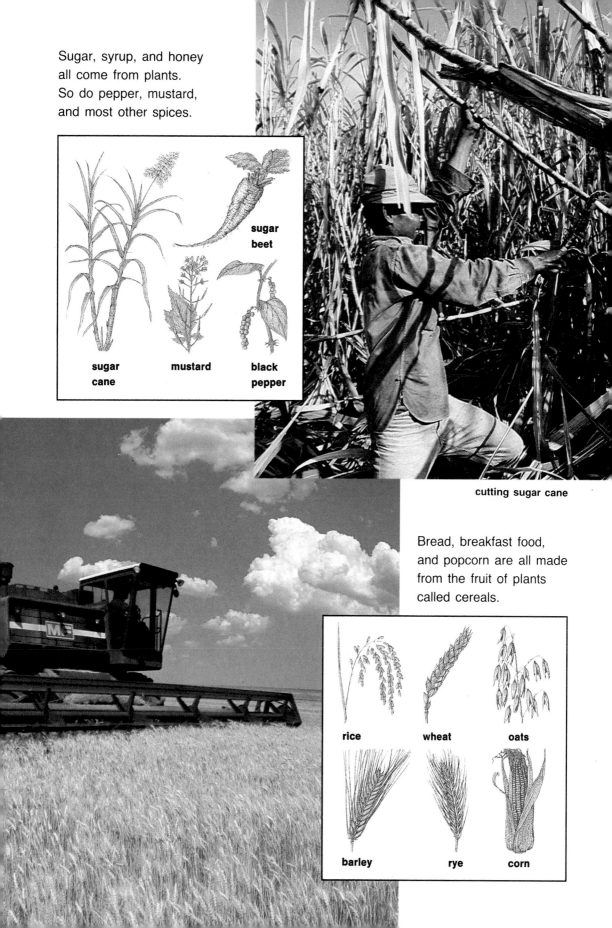

licorice

The flavor of licorice candy comes from this plant's roots.

peppermint

Peppermint candy gets its flavor from this plant.

spearmint

Candy and gum are flavored by oil from this plant.

wintergreen

Wintergreen flavor comes from this plant.

Party treats from plants

Some of our favorite party treats get their flavors from plants.

Do you like licorice candy? Licorice is a flavor made from the root of the licorice plant. Peppermint, spearmint, and wintergreen are flavors made from oils that come from little plants. And vanilla flavor comes from the fruit of an orchid!

We can thank trees for some of our best treats. The nuts that go into fudge, fruit cake, pies, cakes, cookies, and ice cream are all tree seeds! So, of course, are the crunchy cashews and other nuts we eat salted or plain.

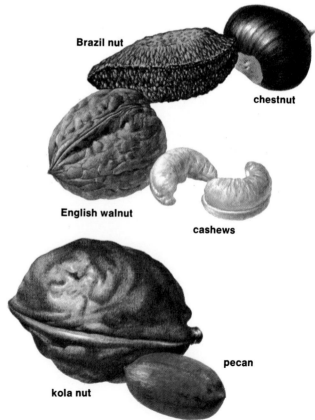

Brazil nut

chestnut

English walnut

cashews

pecan

kola nut

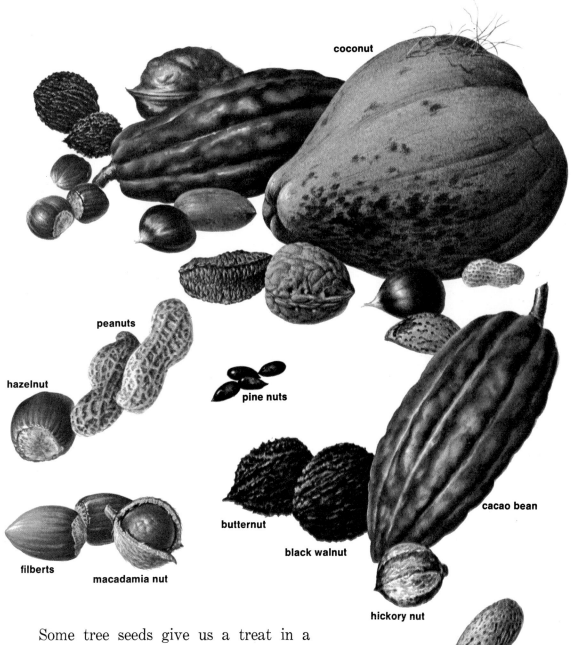

coconut

peanuts

hazelnut

pine nuts

filberts

macadamia nut

butternut

black walnut

cacao bean

hickory nut

almonds

Some tree seeds give us a treat in a different way. We don't eat kola nuts, but from them we get the flavor for fizzy cola drinks. And from cacao beans, which are really tree seeds, too, we get chocolate.

The nut you probably like best—the peanut—isn't a nut at all. In fact, it isn't even a tree seed. It's a kind of pea.

All of these nuts, except the peanut, are the seeds of trees. The peanut is really a pea, and comes from a little leafy plant.

a sawmill

At a sawmill, huge tree trunks are cut into boards. These are used for houses, furniture, and other products.

Baseball bats and hockey sticks

Houses, tables, chairs, and floors,
Rowboats, pencils, desks, and doors,
Baseball bats and hockey sticks,
Boxes for magicians' tricks.
Each and every one of these
Is made of wood that comes from trees!

Dresses, shirts, and tablecloths

Do you have a cotton dress or shirt? Cotton comes from the cotton plant. The seeds are covered with fine fuzz that we twist into thread and weave into cloth.

Is there a linen tablecloth on the table? Linen is made from the flax plant.

cotton plant

harvesting cotton

When cotton fruit is ripe, it pops open. Then the seeds, covered with white fuzz, are harvested.

flax plant

Stalks of flax plants are dried, scraped, and combed into long strips to be spun into thread.

drying flax stalks

Medicines to make you well

If you get sick, a plant may help you get well. Many medicines that doctors give sick people are made from plants.

One of the best medicines is penicillin. It has cured so many kinds of sickness that it has been called a wonder drug. Penicillin comes from plants called molds that grow on bread and fruit.

Different kinds of plants are used to make cough syrups, tonics, and many other medicines that the doctor may give you to take when you don't feel well.

There is one very strange thing about the plants that medicines come from. Most of these plants are poisonous. If you ate one of them you would probably become very sick. You might even die. But when these plants are used in medicines, they help you get well.

People with heart trouble use a medicine made from this plant.

foxglove

penicillium mold

The medicine called penicillin is made from a mold such as this.

Books, tires, and string

The next time you read a book, ride a bicycle, or fly a kite, thank the plants. Without them, you might not be able to do any of those things.

The paper in most books comes from trees. To make paper, wood chips from trees are cooked into a soupy pulp. Then this mixture is squeezed into sheets and dried. Rags of linen or cotton, which also come from plants, are used to make very fine paper.

Bicycle tires and many other things are made from natural or artificial rubber. Natural rubber comes from the milky, white juice of the rubber tree. When the juice is taken from the tree it becomes hard and bouncy. Artificial rubber is made from chemicals, but some of the chemicals come from plants, too.

Kite string is usually made from cotton, which comes from the long threads on seeds of the cotton plant. But most string and rope is made from the veins, called fibers, of long plant leaves. These fibers are removed from the leaves and dried. Then they are twisted together to make rope, string, cord, or twine.

Rubber comes from the juice that flows when a rubber tree is cut.

rubber tree

sisal plants

These swordlike sisal leaves will be used to make string and rope.

Jewels, color, perfume, and music

We get jewelry, perfumes, colors, and even music from plants.

Necklaces and other jewelry are often made of a yellowish rock called amber. And amber came from a plant. Once it was a sticky gum from trees like our pine and spruce trees. This gum turned hard as rock, millions of years ago.

The perfumes people wear probably come from plants, too. The best kinds of perfumes are made of the oil that comes from flowers.

Not long ago, people used the juice of flowers, berries, and bark to give different colors to cloth. Some of these things are still used, but most colors are now made from coal tar. These coal tar dyes come from plants, too, because coal comes from trees that died long ago.

We get music from plants, too. The violins and clarinets in big orchestras and the guitars of folk and rock musicians are made of wood that comes from trees.

amber

Amber is the hardened juice of trees that died millions of years ago. An insect was trapped in this piece of amber before it hardened.

Colors We Get from Plants

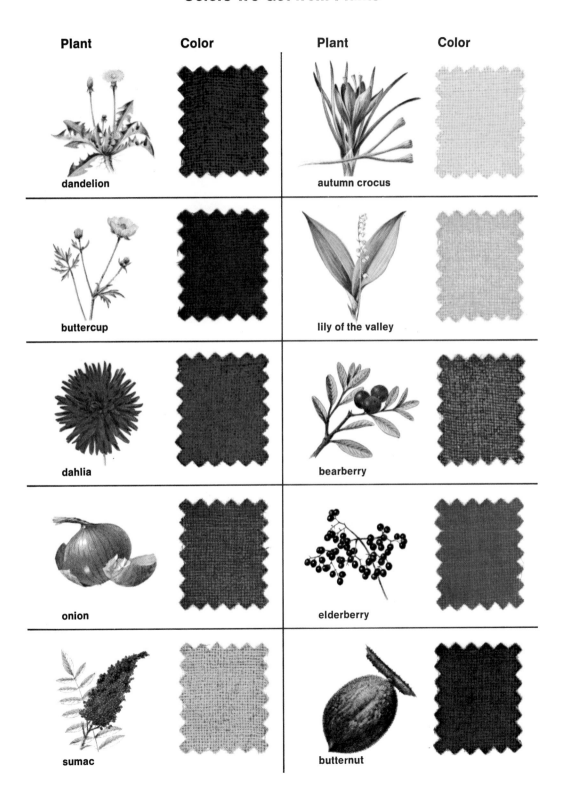

Plant	Color	Plant	Color
dandelion		autumn crocus	
buttercup		lily of the valley	
dahlia		bearberry	
onion		elderberry	
sumac		butternut	

A bright and beautiful world

It's nice to have shady trees around you on a hot, summer day.

It's nice to see the bright faces of flowers nodding at you, and to smell their sweet scent.

It's nice to have cool grass to walk on with bare feet.

Green things make the world seem brighter. We need them around us. Their beauty gives us pleasure and adds to our happiness.

People and Plants

There are many kinds of jobs for people who like to work with plants.

Botanists and other scientists study plants. They look for ways to grow better food plants, to make new things from plants, or to use plants to help cure diseases.

Foresters, gardeners, and other workers plant and care for the flowers and trees you see in parks and gardens and along city streets.

Florists arrange and sell beautiful flowers for special occasions. Growers make it possible for us to plant gardens.

And many artists and photographers make pictures of plants for the books, magazines, and calendars we enjoy.

People who study plants

Do you ever wonder about plants, and how they live and grow? Have you ever taken a flower apart to see what was inside it? If you have wondered about, or done these things, maybe someday you'll be a botanist!

Botanists are scientists who try to find out all about plants. The work of botanists has given us more and better food plants. And it has helped other scientists to make medicine and other useful things from plants.

botanist in a laboratory

Sometimes botanists work outdoors, and sometimes they work in laboratories. This scientist is growing and studying plant cells.

botanist in the desert

Botanists often go to far-off places to study plants in their natural environment.

Botanists study water plants, too. They sometimes work with other scientists to learn which plants can be used for food.

botanist under water

People who find new ways to use plants

Of course, you know that fruits, vegetables, rubber, string, and several kinds of cloth come from plants. But do you know that the clear, smooth cellophane that people sometimes wrap things in comes from plants, too? And so does the margarine you spread on bread.

Scientists called chemists made these things. In laboratories all over the world, chemists are finding new, useful things that can be made from plants.

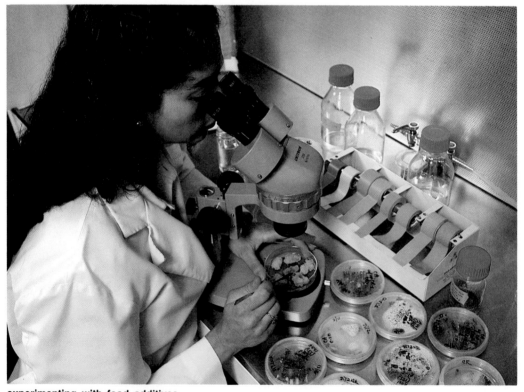

experimenting with food additives

A laboratory technician is doing research to find out about a flavor additive extracted from vanilla beans.

Dr. George Washington Carver

Dr. George Washington Carver was a great
scientist who found many new ways to use
plants. He made more than 100 different
things from corn. And from peanuts he
made more than 300 different things, such
as paper, face cream, flour—and even milk!

People who work with farm plants

If you had a sick pet, you would take it to an animal doctor called a veterinarian. And if you were a farmer with sick plants or poor soil, you would get help from a plant doctor called an agronomist.

Agronomists are scientists who find ways of making soil grow more things, and of making plants larger and healthier. The work they do helps farmers raise more food to feed people around the world.

agronomist in the field

An American agronomist shows farmers in Ghana how to make their crops healthier.

agronomist in a laboratory

This agronomist is testing many
different kinds of soil to see
which is best for these plants.

People who work in forests

Wouldn't it be fun to work in the woods? That's what most foresters do.

There are two kinds of foresters. Some foresters work for a government. They take care of national parks and forests so that people will have places for camping, sightseeing, hunting, and fishing.

Other foresters work in woods that are owned by lumber and paper companies. They raise and care for the trees that are used to make houses, tables, and baseball bats. The paper you write on and the books you read are made from trees that foresters grow.

All foresters protect the trees from insects, animals, and diseases. They make sure that unhealthy trees are replaced with young healthy ones, and that the young trees grow up to be big, healthy trees.

One of a forester's most important jobs is to guard against fire. Lookouts spend days on a lookout station, high on a mountainside, watching for smoke that warns of a fire starting. If they see smoke, they tell the foresters. Then the foresters direct fire fighters in their struggle against a terrible enemy!

However, foresters also set fires! They use small fires to get rid of brush, diseases, and insects, just as you would weed a garden. They control the speed and direction of these fires so that they do not turn into a conflagration—a BIG fire!

foresters at work

New trees are grown to take the place of trees that are cut. The forester is caring for trays of seedlings in a tree nursery.

This sapling has been planted outdoors. The forester is checking the buds to make sure the tree is healthy.

People who help gardens grow

Many people garden for fun. But there are people who work as gardeners and get paid. They work in parks, zoos, and many other public places where there are trees and other plants to care for.

Gardeners and landscapers also work for towns and cities. They are the people who plant and care for the trees, bushes, and beds of flowers that you see along streets and around many public buildings.

landscapers at work

Landscapers often use special tools to dig up trees and replant them in other places.

gardeners at work

These Dutch gardeners are growing tulips for bulbs. The bulbs will be sold to other gardeners all over the world.

People who help us enjoy plants

A florist is an artist and gardener combined. Florists grow and sell plants and flowers. They also make the beautiful bouquets you see at weddings, anniversaries, and on other special occasions.

florist in a greenhouse

Florist shops are beautiful,
All damply green and dimly cool,
And the men who keep them are sure to be
A little baggy about the knee,
With voices pleasant and rather low
From living along with things that grow;
For you can't stay noisy and hurried where
Petal on petal fills the air,
With spiciness, and every tree
Is hung with gayest greenery.
Grocers bustle and butchers shout,
Tradesmen tramp noisily in and out,
But florists are quiet men and kind,
With a sort of fragrance of the mind.

florist arranging flowers ▶

THE FLORIST SHOP
Rachel Field

People who make pictures of plants

Pictures of plants are often needed for magazines, calendars, and books like this one. Many of these pictures are taken by photographers who specialize in photographing plants.

Sometimes, plant pictures are needed that can't be taken by a photographer. Those pictures are made by artists who have made a special study of plants. They can paint pictures that look as real as photographs.

artist Alex Ebel

Alex Ebel specializes in painting pictures of plants and animals that lived millions of years ago. All of the exciting pictures in the section of this book called "Plants of Long Ago" were painted by Mr. Ebel.

photographer David Muench

David Muench enjoys taking pictures that
show the beautiful shapes and designs that
are often found in plants. You can see
some of Mr. Muench's plant photographs on
pages 106, 107, 108, 266, and 272.

True Tales and Tall Tales

Have you ever read a story in which the hero was a plant?

In Scotland, the people tell a story about how thistle plants saved a king.

Have you ever heard about a plant people hunt for with pigs? Or about a girl who turned into a plant? Or about a country that was nearly ruined by a plant?

There are many stories, true and make-believe, about plants. Here are a few of them.

The plant that saved a king

Thistles aren't the sort of flower that people like to pick. They aren't very pretty and they have prickly leaves that hurt you if you touch them. And thistles grow so quickly and thickly that they are pests to farmers.

But the ugly, prickly thistle is an honored plant in Scotland. This is because there is an old Scottish legend that tells how thistles once saved a Scottish king from the Vikings.

Vikings were fierce warriors who came from the northern countries of Sweden, Denmark, and Norway. The Vikings loved war and fighting. They sailed to different parts of the world and attacked towns and castles. They often killed all the people, stole all the riches, and burned everything down.

An old story tells how some Vikings landed in Scotland more than a thousand years ago. During the night they surrounded the Scottish king's castle. Everyone in the castle was asleep. They didn't know the Vikings were about to attack.

All around the castle there was a moat—a deep, wide pit. Moats were usually filled with water, so the Vikings took off their sandals to wade across the moat. But this moat wasn't filled with water. It was dry, and it was filled with thousands of prickly thistles!

When the first barefoot Vikings stepped on those thistles they howled with pain! The noise woke the people in the castle, who were able to defeat the Vikings and chase them away. Today, the thistle is the national emblem of Scotland.

Scottish thistle

The thistle is the national flower of Scotland.

The flower that tells of battles

More than a thousand years ago, says an old French tale, there lived a holy man now known as Saint Leonard. One day he gave away all his money and everything he owned. Then he went to live by himself in a valley in a forest.

But a dragon named Temptation also lived in that valley. This dragon was a huge creature that breathed fire, looked like a snake, and had wings like a bat. The dragon Temptation attacked Saint Leonard, but the holy man chased it away. Saint Leonard and the dragon fought many terrible battles, and the dragon always lost. The holy man chased the beast farther and farther toward the edge of the woods. And, finally, the dragon disappeared forever from the valley.

But a strange thing happened where each of the battles was fought. Wherever drops of Saint Leonard's blood fell to the ground, flowers grew! These flowers were called lilies of the valley, in honor of Saint Leonard's battles in the valley against the dragon Temptation.

lily of the valley

In a French legend, these flowers first grew where drops of a saint's blood fell.

The hunting of the truffle

Truffles, like mushrooms, are a kind of fungus. But unlike mushrooms, truffles grow underground. That makes them hard to find. Truffles are so tasty that people often spend many hours hunting for them. Some people even train animals to help them hunt for truffles. And some of the best truffle hunters are pigs.

Pretend that you're going on a truffle hunt. First, you must go out into the woods where truffles grow. It's a long walk, and if your pig had to walk all the way, it might be too tired to hunt. So you have to carry the pig in your arms. Or, maybe you pull it in a wagon.

When you get to where you think the truffles are,

you tie a rope around the pig's neck. Then you hold on to the other end of the rope and follow the pig as it starts to hunt. It sniffles and snuffles in search of the truffles. When it smells one, it begins to dig.

Pigs like truffles just as much as people do. To keep your pig from eating the truffles, you must quickly drag it away. But you have to give the pig a reward for finding the truffles, or it may stop hunting. So you give it an acorn. Then you tie the pig to a tree and dig up the truffles. They won't look like much—just little, wrinkled, brown balls with warts on them. But people who like the taste of truffles will pay lots of money for them.

truffles

Truffles grow underground.
They are good to eat,
so people hunt for them.

The girl who became a flower

Long ago, the people in Greece believed that the sun was a god named Helios, who drove across the sky in a chariot pulled by four horses. There is a Greek tale about a girl named Clytie who fell in love with Helios. She loved him so much that all she wanted to do was watch as Helios drove across the sky.

All day long, Clytie sat on the ground, watching the sun. She never looked at anything else. She never moved. Even when night came, she stayed where she was, just waiting for the sun to rise.

For nine days and nine nights Clytie did not eat any food. She drank only her tears and the dew from the leaves of near-by plants. And on the tenth day her body took root in the ground. It became a flower stem. Her face became a flower that turned slowly on its stem, still watching the sun move across the sky.

The flower is named the heliotrope. In Greek, this means "turning toward the sun." And true to its name, the beautiful, sweet-scented heliotrope blossom always turns toward the sun.

heliotrope

In Greek legend, this flower was once a girl.

The flower that nearly ruined a country

Imagine paying thousands of dollars for a flower that hasn't even grown yet! That's what many people did about 300 years ago in the Netherlands. Tulips were new to the country, which was called Holland at the time. And rich people were willing to pay lots of money to have tulips in their gardens. Tulips grow from underground buds called bulbs. Many Dutch people saw a chance to make money by selling tulip bulbs.

It takes three to seven years to raise tulip bulbs from seeds. And some people didn't want to wait that long. They wanted money right away, and so they began to sell bulbs before they had them. Tulip bulb growers would sell some bulbs they didn't yet have to others for thousands of dollars in Dutch money. Those people would then sell the bulbs they didn't yet have to others for twice as much.

Tulip bulb prices went higher and higher. Some people even sold their houses to get money to buy tulip bulbs to sell. People traded valuable things for tulip bulbs. One time, a single tulip bulb was sold for 4 cows, 8 pigs, 12 sheep, 2 barrels of butter, 1,000 pounds (450 kilograms) of cheese, 2 big barrels of wine, 4 barrels of beer, 2 wagonloads of wheat, a bed, a suit of clothes, and a large silver cup.

Suddenly, people became afraid to spend so much on tulip bulbs. Prices dropped. People who had bought tulip bulbs couldn't sell them. Many people lost all their money. Others lost their houses. The country of Holland was nearly ruined by tulips.

tulip bulbs

A bulb is an underground bud. The leaves and stem of a tulip grow right out of the bulb.

Saving the Plants

Conservation means "saving things that come from nature"—air, soil, water, animals, and plants.

Plants might not seem to need care, but they do. Plants can get sick, just as people can. Insects can chew their leaves or roots until they die. Fire can turn them into a pile of ashes.

Polluted air from cars and factories can choke the life out of plants. And when ground is dug up for factories, mines, and parking lots, plants lose the space they need to live.

We need to save the plants. They give us beauty and food and fresh air. We couldn't live without them.

That's why conservation is important to the plants—and to you, too.

smut on corn

Smut is a tiny plant called a fungus.
Many of these plants sometimes grow
on corn and make it rot and die.

Deadly enemies

Some deadly enemies of plants lurk in the green kingdom! They are tiny plants called fungi, that look somewhat like cobwebs.

Not all kinds of fungi are deadly. Some live on things that are already decaying, and some live with other plants in ways that are helpful. But some fungi are plant killers. They fasten themselves to plants and use them as food. The fungi grow and multiply, causing the other plants to become slimy and rotten. These plant-killing fungi have nasty-sounding names such as smut, blight, rust, and mildew.

Fungi can harm even the largest plants. Once, beautiful chestnut trees grew everywhere in North America. Most of them are gone now. They were killed by blight.

Can fungi cause trouble for people? They certainly can. In Ireland, in the 1840's, a blight attacked the potato crop. More than 750,000 people starved to death, because potatoes were their chief food.

Most plants are helpless when fungi attack them. But people can help plants fight fungi. Scientists have found chemicals that help keep plants from being attacked. They have also learned how to raise plants that can't be harmed by fungi. Scientists are still working to find better ways to save plants from these deadly enemies.

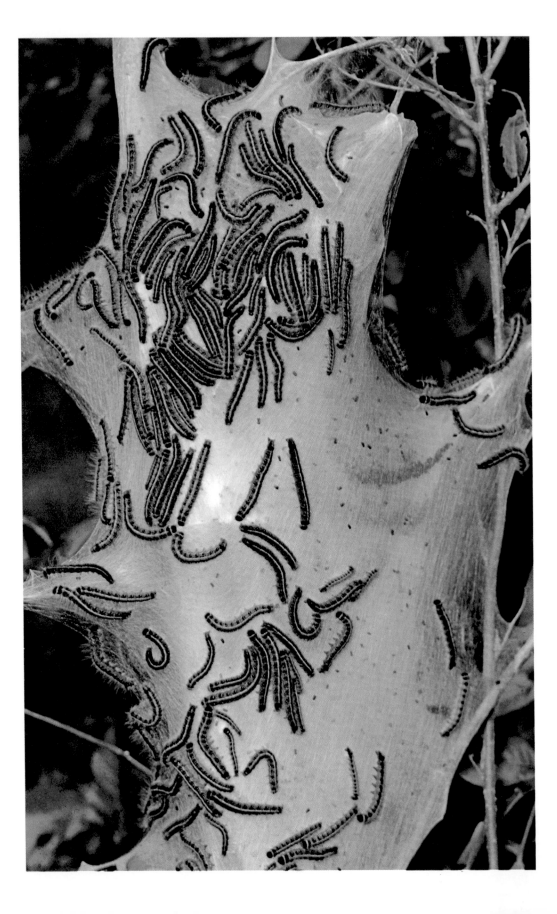

Insect enemies

Suppose you could make yourself as tiny as an insect. Then, suppose you sat on a leaf in a garden and were very still. You would probably hear a munching, crunching noise all around you. For, all summer long, day and night, billions of insects chew away at plants.

Many insects are truly plant enemies. And they're our enemies, too, because their food is often the same as ours—corn, wheat, tomatoes, potatoes, and fruit.

There are several ways to protect plants from insects. Some people use poison sprays, but many of these sprays are dangerous. Gardeners and farmers know that one of the best ways to protect plants from insects is with other insects.

Once, little insects called aphids were damaging alfalfa crops in California. The farmers turned thousands of ladybugs loose in their fields. The ladybugs gobbled up the aphids and saved the crops.

Using insects to fight insects is the safest way to protect plants. Scientists are looking for other ways. Getting rid of harmful insect enemies is important. But it has to be done with care. All insects, even those that attack plants, help maintain the balance of nature.

tent caterpillars

Tent caterpillars are deadly enemies of plants. A nest of tent caterpillars will often eat all the buds or young leaves on a tree. When this happens, the tree will die.

The enemy in the air

Imagine a world that is plain, even ugly —a world without beauty. Imagine a world in which most of the trees are dead. Many other plants are small and twisted. Leaves and flowers are spotted with disease. And fruits, such as grapes, apples, peaches, and plums, can't grow.

It wouldn't be a very nice world. But many scientists fear that's what our world is going to be like some day—if we don't do something about air pollution!

Air pollution can make you cough. It also makes your eyes water and sting. But it does far worse things to plants. It kills trees. It keeps flowers from budding. It spoils fruits and vegetables.

Air pollution is a very serious problem. But scientists and many other people are working on it. They're trying to clean up the air and keep it clean, for the sake of people *and* plants.

damaged aspen leaves

These leaves were damaged
by fumes from cars and trucks.

Air pollution, caused by cars
and trucks, is killing this
pine tree near a highway in
Hämeenlinna, Finland.

dying tree near a highway

mine or national park?

From open-pit mines such as the one in the top picture, we get a useful and important metal—copper. But this kind of mine destroys both land and plants. The bottom picture shows a place where valuable metals have been found. Some people want to dig an open-pit mine here. Others, who want to see the land stay the way it is, are trying to have the area declared a national park.

The most dangerous enemies

Plants and animals have enemies that are more dangerous than any others. Their most dangerous enemies are people.

People are the only living creatures that have ever caused other living creatures to become extinct. The dodo, the passenger pigeon, and the great auk, all hunted and killed by people, are gone forever.

Now, the same kind of thing is happening in the Green Kingdom. Plants need land to grow. But people need roads, houses, factories, mines, shopping centers, and parking lots. So trees are chopped down, and land is cleared and built on and paved. Little by little, the great forests, the coastal marshlands, and the wide, rolling prairies are disappearing.

We need the things that can be built on the land or taken out of it. But if we change too much land, we may upset the balance of nature. If this happens, people might someday become extinct. People also need the natural beauty of unspoiled land. Without this beauty, people might lose their very love of life.

How can we solve this problem? In one way, the answer is simple. We must save some land and use other land. But which land should we save, and which land can we use? People in government, industry, and private groups are trying to find a good answer to this difficult question.

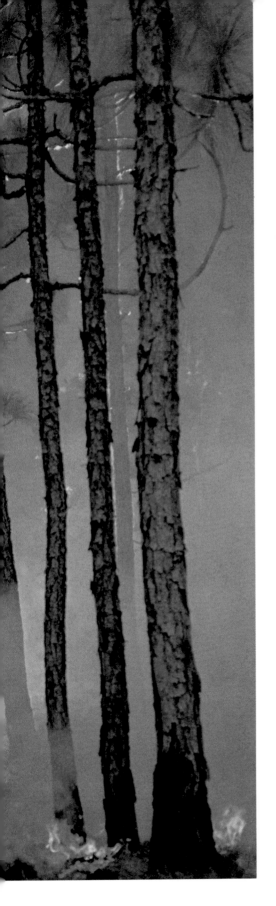

Fire!

The forest rangers are worried. The weather is hot and there has been no rain for a long time. They know the forest is as dry as sawdust. It would take only a tiny spark to turn the whole forest into a roaring, raging sea of fire!

From their watchtower high above the trees, the rangers see a thin spiral of smoke. Fire! There's a fire in the forest!

A quick call for help goes out. Fire fighters rush to the blaze in trucks. Working quickly, they battle the blaze with streams of water and shovelfuls of soil. They chop down trees and dig up the ground to keep the fire from spreading.

Overhead, airplanes swoop over the fire, dropping water and chemicals on it. From other planes come fire fighters called smoke jumpers. They parachute into places that the fire fighters on the ground can't reach easily.

At last, after hours, or perhaps even days, the fire is out. Thousands of trees that might have become blackened stumps have been saved.

A forest is long in growing, but its ashes are made in a moment.

SENECA

planting trees

You can help save the green kingdom by planting new plants where they are needed. These children are planting healthy young trees on the grounds of their school.

collecting wastepaper

Wastepaper can help save trees! It can be sold to mills that will make new paper from it. Then fewer trees will have to be cut down to be made into paper.

What you can do to help

You may think there's not much you can do to help save plants. But there are lots of things you can do! Here are just a few.

Save your family's old newspapers and wastepaper. Boy Scouts, Girl Scouts, and other groups often collect old paper. It can be sent to places that will make new paper from it. This means that fewer trees will be cut down to be made into paper.

If you have a lawn, rake the leaves that fall on it in autumn. Don't burn them. That pollutes the air. Instead, rake them into a pile that's flat on top and leave them where rain can soak into them. They will rot and turn into dark, muddy-looking humus. Spread the humus on your lawn and it will make the soil richer for the grass and other plants.

Sometimes you can help plants by not doing things.

Don't peel bark from trees. The outside bark protects a tree from insects and fungus enemies. The inner bark moves food from the leaves to the roots. Peeling off a tree's bark may cause the tree to die.

When you pick wild flowers, don't take them all. Let some grow so that they can make seeds. Then, the next year, there will be many more wild flowers for everyone to enjoy.

Look for a Lovely Thing

All around you, the beauty of the green kingdom fills the world.

Meadows in spring are carpets of green and gold and pink. Deserts are splashed with bright blossoms after rain. Woods glow with fiery autumn reds and purples. Snow blankets the prairies in white and silver.

There is beauty in a flower hung with raindrops. There is beauty in a leaf silvered with frost. There is beauty in bark and branches, in stems and seeds.

Beauty is all around you. The green kingdom makes the world a lovely place.

Look for a lovely thing and you will find it,
It is not far—
It never will be far.

from NIGHT
Sara Teasdale

timothy and brome grass
in moonlight

fungi

iris

O Lord, how manifold are thy works!
In wisdom hast thou made them all:
The earth is full of thy riches.

PSALMS 104:24

squirreltail grass

To every thing there is a season,
And a time to every purpose under heaven:
A time to be born and a time to die . . .

ECCLESIASTES 3:1–2

black oak leaves

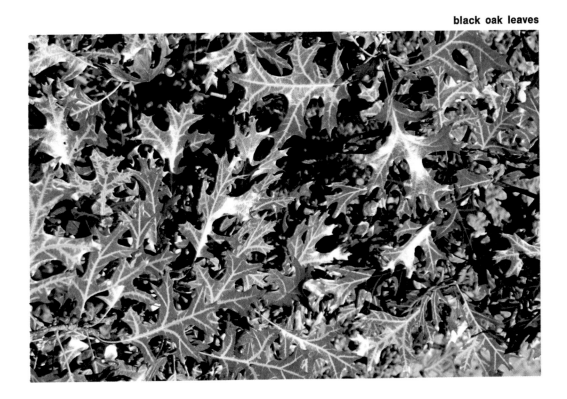

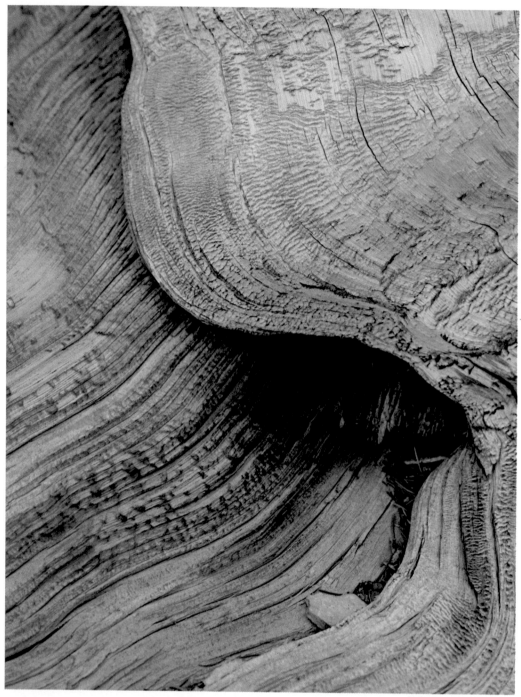

bristlecone pine bole

We paused amid the pines that stood
   The giants of the waste,
Tortured by storms to shapes as rude
   As serpents interlaced . . .

from THE RECOLLECTION
Percy Bysshe Shelley

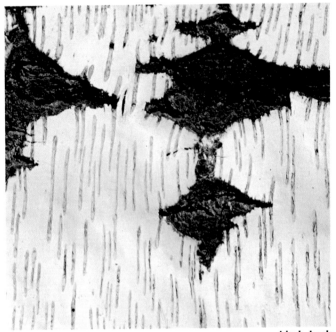

birch bark

"Lay aside your cloak, O Birch-tree!
Lay aside your white-skin wrapper,
For the Summer-time is coming,
and the sun is warm in heaven,
And you need no white-skin wrapper!"

from THE SONG OF HIAWATHA
Henry Wadsworth Longfellow

A thing of beauty is a joy for ever:
Its loveliness increases; it will never
Pass into nothingness . . .

From ENDYMION
John Keats

salsify

Books to Read

If you enjoy learning about plants, you'll find many interesting books about them. The books listed here are only a sampling. Your school or public library will have more.

Ages 5 to 8

Between Cattails by Terry Tempest Williams (Scribner, 1985)
Cattails are tall plants with brown furry spikes that live in marshes. The book will tell you all about cattails and other plants and animals that live in marshes.

A Book of Vegetables by Harriet L. Sobol (Putnam, 1984)
You may find vegetables more interesting at the dinner table after learning about them and the plants they grow on.

Discovering Trees by Douglas Florian (Scribner, 1986)
You see trees every day, but how much do you really know about them? This book helps you to identify some trees and tells how they grow.

Farming and Land: Modern Farmers and Their Machines by Jerry Bushey (Carolrhoda, 1987)
If you like machines, you will probably enjoy this book about farming machines. It explains how machines are used on a farm.

From Spore to Spore by Jerome Wexler (Dodd, 1985)
This book describes the life cycle of ferns and tells how you can raise them.

Grass and Grasshoppers by Rose Wyler (Messner, 1990)
If you like to do experiments, this is the book for you! There are experiments on almost every page that have to do with grass and some of the animals that "hop" through it.

In My Garden: A Child's Gardening Book by Helen and Kelly Oechsli (Macmillan, 1985)
If you want a vegetable garden of your own, this is the guide you need to get started.

In the Forest by Jim Arnosky (Lothrop, 1989)
This book is a collection of paintings of forests, with explanations of what each painting includes.

Mushrooms by Millicent E. Selsam (Morrow, 1986)
Are all plants in the green kingdom green? Not the mysterious mushroom!

There Once Was A Tree by Natalia Romanova (Dial Press, 1985)
What happens when an old tree is split by lightning? The answer to this question is explained in words and beautiful pictures in this book.

Plants That Never Ever Bloom by Ruth Heller (Grosset, 1984)
The author introduces you to a group of plants that don't flower.

Ages 9 and Up

An Apple Tree Through the Year by Claudia Schnieper (Carolrhoda, 1987)
This book follows an apple tree's life from winter through the seasons to fall, when the tree is filled with ripe apples.

Earthworms, Dirt, and Rotten Leaves: An Exploration in Ecology by Molly McLaughlin (Atheneum, 1986)
Earthworms are an important part of the community. This book includes experiments that you can do with earthworms so you will better understand them.

A Forest Year by Carol Lerner (Morrow, 1987)
A forest changes throughout the four seasons of the year. Read how these changes affect the plants and animals that call the forest home.

From Flower to Flower: Animals and Pollination by Patricia Lauber (Crown, 1986)
Many flowers need bees or other insects to help them make seeds. Learn how animals help with the process of pollination.

How Did We Find Out About Photosynthesis? by Isaac Asimov (Walker, 1989)
This book not only explains what photosynthesis is, but also tells how it was discovered and explained through the ages.

How Leaves Change by Sylvia A. Johnson (Lerner, 1986)
If you have ever wondered what makes leaves turn such beautiful colors in the fall, read this book.

Moonseed and Mistletoe: A Book of Poisonous Wild Plants by Carol Lerner (Morrow, 1988)
Some poisonous plants cause minor skin rashes—others cause death. Find out about the most common poisonous wild plants.

One Day in the Prairie by Jean Craighead George (Crowell, 1986)
The author of this book describes the importance of prairie grass to all living things on the prairie.

Plant Families by Carol Lerner (Morrow, 1989)
Did you know that broccoli, cabbage, and turnips are all members of the mustard plant family? This beautifully illustrated book is full of information about how plants are related.

Potato by Barrie Watts (Silver Burdett, 1987)
Full-page photographs and written explanations show how the potato plant develops from a shoot to a full-grown plant with the tubers, or underground food-storing stems, that we eat.

Rice by Sylvia Johnson (Lerner, 1985)
Rice is the basic food crop for one-half of the people in the world. This book discusses the planting and harvesting of this important plant.

Tiger Lilies and Other Beastly Plants by Elizabeth Ring (Walker, 1984)
Can you think of a plant that reminds you of a cat? How about a pussy willow? This book describes several kinds of plants that remind people in some way of animals.

Wheat: The Golden Harvest by Dorothy Hinshaw Patent (Putnam, 1987)
The author refers to wheat as "our most important food." She tells about the different varieties of wheat and describes the processes of planting and harvesting wheat for food.

New Words

Here are some of the words you've met in this book. They may be new to you. Many of them are words you'll meet again in other books—so they're good words to know. Some of them are flower names that may be hard for you to pronounce. Next to each word you are shown how to say it correctly: acid (AS ihd). The part of the word shown in capital letters is said a little more loudly. Under each word, the meaning is given in a complete sentence.

acid (AS ihd)
An acid is a chemical substance strong enough to dissolve things.

agronomist (uh GRAHN uh mihst)
An agronomist is a person who studies how to improve the soil so that crops can grow better.

algae (AL jee)
Algae are green plants without stems, roots, or leaves. They live in water or moist soil and make their own food.

alyssum (uh LIHS uhm)
Alyssum is a plant of the mustard family. It has small yellow, pink, rose, or white flowers.

annual (AN yoo uhl)
An annual is a plant that lives only one year.

anther (AN thuhr)
The anther is a tiny sack on a stem inside a flower. The anthers hold the pollen.

biome (BY ohm)
In nature, a place where certain kinds of plants and animals live together is called a biome. The climate limits the kinds of plants and animals that can live there.

botanist (BAHT uh nihst)
A botanist is a person who studies plants.

broccoli (BRAHK uh lee)
Broccoli is an annual plant that is eaten as a vegetable.

bulrush (BUL ruhsh)
Bulrush is a tall, slender plant that grows in or near water.

cacao (kuh KAY oh)
The cacao is a kind of evergreen tree. Cocoa and chocolate are made from its seeds.

calamus (KAL uh muhs)
Calamus is a plant with long, sword-shaped leaves.

carbon dioxide (KAHR buhn dy AHK syd)
Carbon dioxide is a heavy, colorless gas that does not have an odor.

carotene (KAR uh teen) or
carotin (KAR uh tihn)
Carotene is a red or yellow color found in plants and animals. Carrots have carotene.

cauliflower (KAW luh flow uhr)
Cauliflower is an annual plant that is eaten as a vegetable.

celery (SEHL uh ree)
Celery is a plant with crisp, long stalks eaten as a vegetable or in salads.

cell (sehl)
A cell is the smallest part of all living things.

cereal (SIHR ee uhl)
Cereal is any plant, such as wheat or oats, that produces a grain used for food.

chemist (KEHM ihst)
A chemist is a person who studies substances to find out what they are made of, how they act, and how they change.

chlorophyll (KLAWR uh fihl)
Chlorophyll is the green coloring matter made by plants.

chloroplast (KLAWR uh plast)
A chloroplast is a tiny, round package of color found in some plant cells.

chrysanthemum (kruh SAN thuh muhm)
Chrysanthemum is a plant with flowers that bloom in the autumn.

cinnamon (SIHN uh muhn)
Cinnamon is a spice made from the bark of a tropical laurel tree.

coleus (KOH lee uhs)
Coleus is a plant with showy, colorful leaves that belongs to the mint family.

conifer (KOH nuh fuhr)
A conifer is any of a large group of trees and shrubs, most of which are evergreen and bear cones.

conservation (KAHN suhr VAY shun)
Conservation is the protection and wise use of natural resources—water, air, soil, minerals, plants, and animals.

cypress (SY pruhs)
Cypress is an evergreen tree with dark green, overlapping leaves, and hard wood.

dahlia (DAL yuh)
Dahlia is a tall plant with large flowers that bloom in the autumn.

delphinium (dehl FIHN ee uhm)
Delphinium is a plant that has blue flowers on a tall stalk.

diatom (DY uh tahm)
A diatom is a tiny water plant.

digest (duh JEHST or dy JEHST)
To digest is to break down food so that it can be used. A plant or animal digests food by dissolving it inside itself.

fiber (FY buhr)
A fiber is a long, threadlike piece of a plant.

fungus (FUHNG guhs)
A fungus is a plant without flowers, leaves, or chlorophyll. Two or more such plants are called fungi (FUN jy).

gall (gawl)
A gall is a lump that forms on leaves, stems, or roots of plants where they have been hurt by insects or fungi.

geranium (juh RAY nee uhm)
Geranium is a plant with sweet-smelling leaves and pretty flowers.

ginkgo (GIHNG koh)
Ginkgo is a large tree with leaves shaped like little fans.

gladiolus (GLAD ee OH luhs)
Gladiolus is a plant with long leaves and large, handsome flowers.

heliotrope (HEE lee uh trohp)
Heliotrope is a plant with sweet-smelling flowers that range from light purple to dark blue in color. It is also a name for any plant whose flowers turn to follow the sun.

hepatica (hih PAT uh kuh)
Hepatica is a plant with flowers that bloom in early spring.

herb (urb)
An herb is a plant whose leaves or other parts are used for medicine, seasoning, food, or perfume.

horticulturist (hawr tuh KUHL chuhr ihst)
A horticulturist is a person skilled in growing flowers, fruits, vegetables, and other plants.

humus (HYOO muhs)
Humus is a black or dark-brown soil made by the rotting of leaves and other parts of plants.

hyacinth (HY uh sihnth)
The hyacinth is a plant with bunches of little bell-shaped flowers on the ends of long stalks.

Joshua tree (JAHSH u uh tree)
The Joshua tree is a small tree that grows in the desert.

lichen (LY kuhn)
Lichen is fungi and algae plants that are growing together so that they look like one plant. It looks like moss.

macadamia (mak uh DAY mee uh)
Macadamia is a tree or shrub that grows in Hawaii. The nuts are good to eat.

maize (mayz)
Maize is Indian corn.

mineral (MIHN uhr uhl)
A mineral is a substance that is not animal or vegetable.

mistletoe (MIHS uhl toh)
Mistletoe is a plant with small, waxy, white berries and yellow flowers.

oleander (OH lee AN duhr)
Oleander is a poisonous evergreen.

orchid (AWR kihd)
Orchid is a plant with beautiful flowers. The flowers of most orchids have a central petal with an unusual shape.

ovule (OH vyool)
The ovule is the part of a plant that develops into a seed.

oxygen (AHK suh juhn)
Oxygen is a gas without color or odor. It is part of the air that you breathe.

papyrus (puh PY ruhs)
Papyrus is a tall water plant once used to make paper.

penicillin (PEHN uh SIHL ihn)
Penicillin is a medicine that was first made from a green mold.

penicillium (PEHN uh SIHL ee uhm)
Penicillium is the kind of mold used to make penicillin.

perennial (puh REHN ee uhl)
A perennial is a plant that lives more than two years.

poinsettia (poyn SEHT ee uh)
Poinsettia is a plant with a small flower surrounded by large red leaves that look like petals.

pollen (PAHL uhn)
Pollen is a yellowish powder formed in the anthers of flowers. When pollen reaches a flower's ovule, a seed is usually formed.

pollinate (PAHL uh nayt)
To pollinate is to carry pollen from one flower to another.

rhubarb (ROO bahrb)
Rhubarb is a plant whose thick stalks are used for making pies and sauces.

salsify (SAL suh fy)
Salsify is a purple-flowered plant; its roots are eaten as a vegetable.

sassafras (SAS uh fras)
Sassafras is a slender American tree; its bark is used in making medicine, candy, and tea.

seedling (SEED lihng)
A seedling is a young plant grown from a seed.

sensitive (SEHN suh tihv)
Anything that responds to an outside force (such as light) is thought of as being sensitive.

sequoia (sih KWOY uh)
Sequoia is a very tall evergreen tree.

sisal (SIHS uhl)
Sisal is a strong fiber used for making rope or twine.

spore (spawr)
A spore is a single cell that comes from a plant and can develop into a new plant.

stigma (STIHG muh)
The stigma is the part of a plant that receives the pollen.

sumac (SOO mak)
Sumac is a bush with divided leaves; some kinds are poisonous to the touch.

sycamore (SIHK uh mawr)
Sycamore is a large, common shade tree; its fruit looks like a small, greenish ball.

tamarack (TAM uh rak)
Tamarack is a tree of the pine family with small cones and needles that fall off in the autumn.

tendril (TEHN druhl)
A tendril is the threadlike part of a climbing plant that attaches itself to something and helps support the plant.

thistle (THIHS uhl)
Thistle is a plant that is thickly covered with sharp points.

truffle (TRUHF uhl)
Truffle is a fungus that can be eaten; it grows underground.

tundra (TUHN druh)
The tundra is a great, treeless plain in a cold place, such as the area just south of the ice and snow that surrounds the North Pole.

xanthophyll (ZAN thuh fihl)
Xanthophyll is the yellow color found in autumn leaves.

Illustration acknowledgments

The publishers of *Childcraft* gratefully acknowledge the courtesy of the following artists, photographers, publishers, agencies, and corporations for illustrations in this volume. Page numbers refer to two-page spreads. The words *"(left),"* *"(center),"* *"(top),"* *"(bottom),"* and *"(right)"* indicate position on the spread. All illustrations are the exclusive property of the publishers of *Childcraft* unless names are marked with an asterisk (*).

1: *(top left)* K. Harris, The Nature Conservancy *; *(top right)* Alan Pitcairn from Grant Heilman *; *(center left)* Torkel Korling *; *(center right)* Les Blacklock, Tom Stack & Assoc. *; *(bottom left and right)* Norman Weaver

4-19: Gyo Fujikawa

20-25: James Teason

26-27: *(top right)* George Suyeoka; *(bottom)* James Teason

28-29: *(left)* Nigel Alexander (Specs Art Agency); *(right)* George Suyeoka

30-31: *(top right)* George Suyeoka; *(bottom)* James Teason

32-37: George Suyeoka

38-39: *(left)* Angela Lumley (Specs Art Agency); *(top center)* Adrian Davies, Bruce Coleman Ltd. *; *(bottom center)* A. J. Deane, Bruce Coleman Ltd. *

40-41: *(top left)* Hermann Eisenbeiss, Photo Researchers *; *(center left)* Jerome Wexler, NAS *; *(right)* James Teason

42-43: *(left)* Geoff Doré, Bruce Coleman Ltd. *; *(right)* James Teason

44-45: Harold Hungerford *

46-47: *(left)* Robert Keys *; *(right)* Edward S. Ross *

48-49: Jean Helmer

50-51: Irvin L. Oakes, NAS *

52-53: *(top left)* Sven Samelius *; *(center left)* Russ Kinne, Photo Researchers *; *(bottom left)* Ken Brate, Photo Researchers *; *(top right)* Walter Chandoha *; *(bottom right)* Grant Heilman *; art, Jean Helmer

54-55: Russ Kinne, Photo Researchers *

56-57: *(top left)* Torkel Korling *; *(center left)* Jane Burton, Bruce Coleman Ltd. *; *(bottom left)* Edward S. Ross *; *(top right and center)* Torkel Korling *; *(bottom right)* Edward S. Ross *; art left, Jane Pickering (Linden Artists Ltd.); art right, Jean Helmer

58-59: Les Blacklock, Tom Stack & Assoc. *

60-61: *(top left)* Torkel Korling *; *(bottom left)* Harold Hungerford, Tom Stack & Associates *; *(top center)* Edward S. Ross *; *(bottom center)* G. D. Plage, Bruce Coleman Ltd. *; *(top right)* E. R. Degginger *; *(bottom right)* Torkel Korling *; art left, David Thompson (Linden Artists Ltd.); art right, Jean Helmer

62-63: Ron Church *

64-65: *(top left)* Joan E. Rahn *; *(bottom left and left center)* Ron Church, Tom Stack & Associates *; *(bottom center)* Walter Dawn *; *(top right)* Eileen Tanson, Tom Stack & Associates *; *(right center)* Carlson Ray, Photo Researchers *; bottom art, David Thompson (Linden Artists Ltd.); art right, Jean Helmer

66-67: Gale Belinky, Photo Researchers *

68-69: *(top left and left center)* Noble Proctor, Photo Researchers *; *(bottom left and bottom right)* Les Blacklock, Tom Stack & Associates *; *(center)* Sven Samelius *; art left, David Thompson (Linden Artists Ltd.); art right, Jean Helmer

70-71: Loren McIntyre, Woodfin Camp, Inc. *

72-73: *(top left)* Russ Kinne, Photo Researchers *; *(left center)* Jacques Jangoux *; *(center)* G. R. Roberts *; *(bottom and top right)* Edward S. Ross *; art left and top right, Jane Pickering (Linden Artists Ltd.); art right, Jean Helmer

74-75: Gene Ahrens, Bruce Coleman Inc. *

76-77: *(top left)* Edward S. Ross *; *(center)* Harold Hungerford *; *(left center)* Alan Pitcairn from Grant Heilman *; *(bottom)* Walter Chandoha *; *(top right)* R. H. Lynam, Tom Stack & Associates *; *(right center)* Andy Bernhaut, Photo Researchers *; *(bottom right)* Paolo Koch, Photo Researchers *; art left, Jane Pickering (Linden Artists Ltd.); art right, Jean Helmer

78-79: Steve and Dolores McCutcheon *

80-81: *(top left and bottom center)* Jen and Des Bartlett, Bruce Coleman Ltd. *; *(top center)* Russ Kinne, Photo Researchers *; *(top right and center right)* Steve and Dolores McCutcheon *; *(center left)* Sven Samelius *; art, Jean Helmer

82-83: David Muench *

84-85: *(top left)* V. B. Sheffer, NAS *; *(left center)* Klaus W. Büth, Anthony-Verlag *; *(center)* Sven Samelius *; *(bottom left)* Torkel Korling *; *(top right)* Heinz Schrempp *; *(bottom right)* Boyd Norton *; art left, Pat Harby (Linden Artists Ltd.); art right, Jean Helmer

86-87: Harry McNaught

88-89: *(left)* Childcraft photos; *(right)* Edward S. Ross *

90-91: *(left)* Bendel, Zefa Picture Library *; *(inset left)* Anheuser-Busch, Inc. *; *(right)* R. Bond, Zefa Picture Library *; art, Peter Geissler (Specs Art Agency)

92-93: Lou Bory

94-95: *(top left and top right)* Jane Burton, Bruce Coleman Ltd. *; *(bottom left)* E. R. Degginger *; *(right center)* Russ Kinne, Photo Researchers *; *(right)* Michel Viard, Bruce Coleman Ltd. *

96-97: *(top left)* Walter Chandoha *; *(bottom left)* Walter Dawn *; *(right)* Lou Bory

98-99: *(top left)* Charles Belinky, Photo Researchers *; *(top center)* Grant Heilman *; *(right)* E. R. Degginger *; *(bottom)* Victor Englebert, Photo Researchers *

100-103: Harry McNaught

104-105: Edward S. Ross *; *(bottom right)* Karl Weidmann *

106-107: David Muench *

108-109: *(left)* David Muench *; *(right)* from *Island Life* by Sherwin Carlquist, © 1965 by Sherwin Carlquist. Reproduced by permission of Doubleday & Company, Inc. *

110-113: Betty Fraser

114-115: Hugh Spencer, NAS *

116-117: *(left)* Runk/Schoenberger from Grant Heilman *; *(right)* © Larry West *; art, Betty Fraser

118-119: *(left)* Harold Hungerford *; *(right)* Betty Fraser

120-121: *(left)* Betty Fraser; *(right)* M. E. Warren *

122-123: *(top)* Don Renfro, NAS *; *(left)* Alvin E. Staffan, NAS *; *(center)* Edward S. Ross *; *(right)* Richard Parker, NAS *; *(bottom)* Larry Moon, Tom Stack & Associates *

124-125: *(top left)* Marcia W. Griffen, Earth Scenes *; *(bottom left)* © Patti Murray, Earth Scenes *; art, Betty Fraser

126-127: *(left)* Betty Fraser; *(right)* © Roger Wilmshurst, Bruce Coleman Ltd. *

128-129: *(left)* John Neel, Tom Stack & Associates *; *(right)* Betty Fraser

130-131: *(top left)* Betty Fraser; *(bottom left)* W. Atlee Burpee & Co. *; *(right)* © Eric Crichton, Bruce Coleman Ltd. *

132-133: *(bottom left and top center)* E. R. Degginger *; *(top left)* Jane Burton, Photo Researchers *; *(center)* Joan E. Rahn *; *(bottom center)* Alvin E. Staffan, NAS *; *(top right)* Edward S. Ross *; *(bottom right)* C. G. Maxwell, Photo Researchers *

134-135: *(left and top left)* Walter Chandoha *; *(top right)* Veryl Schiebner, Photo Researchers *; *(bottom left)* Hoppock Associates *; *(bottom right)* Gene Ahrens, Bruce Coleman Inc. *

136-137: Jack Endevelt

138-139: *(top right)* Josephine Von Miklos *; *(bottom)* C. William Randall

140-141: Wayne Stuart

142-143: *(left)* Wayne Stuart; *(right)* Peter Geissler (Specs Art Agency)

144-145: Miller Services *

146-147: *(left)* Rapho Guillumette *; *(right)* Wayne Stuart

148-153: C. William Randall

154-155: Wayne Stuart

156-159: C. William Randall

160-161: Charles Raymond

162-163: *(left)* Hermann Eisenbeiss *; *(top)* Gottscho-Shleisner, Inc. *; *(bottom right)* Longwood Gardens, Kennett Square, Pa. *

164-165: *(left)* Frances Bannett, DPI *; *(top right)* T. M. McCausland, Bruce Coleman Inc. *; *(bottom right)* Ronny Jaques, Photo Researchers *

166-167: *(top left)* John Gajda, DPI *; *(top right)* Van Bucher, Photo Researchers *; *(bottom)* William McQuitty *

168-169: *(top and bottom right)* William McQuitty *; *(bottom left)* Van Bucher, Photo Researchers *

170-187: Robert Keys

188-189: *(left)* Grant Heilman *; *(right)* Rutherford Platt *

190-191: *(left)* © Miro Vintoniv, Stock Boston *; *(right)* Lyle Lamont

192-197: Alex Ebel

198-199: *(left)* Alex Ebel; *(right)* Al Gentry, Missouri Botanical Garden *

200-201: *(left)* Alex Ebel; *(right)* © Hans Reinhard, Bruce Coleman Ltd. *

202-203: *(top left, top center, and bottom right)* *Childcraft* photos courtesy Field Museum of Natural History, Chicago; *(bottom center)* *World Book* photo

204-205: Robert Keys

206-207: *(left)* The Nature Conservancy *; *(right)* Laura D'Argo

208-209: Norman Weaver

210-211: *(left)* Deere & Co. *; *(top right)* © Alain Compost, Bruce Coleman Ltd. *; art, Norman Weaver

212-213: Norman Weaver

214-215: *(top left)* Georgia-Pacific *; *(bottom left)* Fritz Henle, Photo Researchers *; *(top right)* Mississippi Agricultural and Industrial Board *; art, Norman Weaver

216-217: *(top left)* W. Atlee Burpee & Co. *; *(bottom left)* Pfizer Inc. *; *(top right)* © John Fennell, Bruce Coleman Ltd. *; *(bottom right)* © George H. Harrison from Grant Heilman *

218-219: *(left)* *World Book* photo; *(right)* Norman Weaver

220-221: Charles Stone *

222-223: Jack Endevelt

224-225: *(left)* Runk/Shoenberger from Grant Heilman *; *(top right)* Frans Lanting, Bruce Coleman Ltd. *; *(bottom right)* Flip Schulke, Black Star *

226-227: *(left)* © Lawrence Migdale *; *(right)* Tuskegee Institute *

228-229: *(left)* Peter Larsen *; *(right)* Walter Dawn *

230-231: Georgia-Pacific *

232-233: *(left)* Charles Fiore Nurseries, Inc. *; *(right)* Miller Services *

234-235: *(left)* Three Lions *; *(right)* © Wendy Neefus, Earth Scenes *

236-237: *(left)* John Anthos *; *(right)* David Muench *

238-239: Monica Laimgruber

240-241: *(left)* William Stobbs; *(right)* Pamela Harper *

242-243: *(left)* Klaus Winter and Helmut Bischoff; *(right)* W. Atlee Burpee & Co. *

244-245: *(left)* Susi Weigel; *(right)* Michel Viard, Bruce Coleman Ltd. *

246-247: *(right)* W. Atlee Burpee & Co. *; art, Pauline Baynes

248-249: *(top)* Babs Van Wely; *(bottom)* W. Atlee Burpee & Co. *

250-251: Lyle Lamont

252-253: Linda Hungerford *

254-255: Louis Quitt, NAS *

256-257: *(top)* University of Illinois at Urbana *; *(bottom)* © Tom McHugh, Photo Researchers *

258-259: Boyd Norton *

260-261: Jack Dermid, Bruce Coleman Inc. *

262-263: *(top)* © Lawrence Migdale *; *(bottom)* Tom Myers, Tom Stack & Associates *

264-265: Dan Morrill from Vince Kamin *

266-267: *(top left)* John Neel, Tom Stack & Associates *; *(bottom left)* Zaner Miller, Tom Stack & Associates *; *(right)* Joan E. Rahn from Vince Kamin *

268-269: *(left)* David Muench *; *(right)* James Milmoe *

270-271: Bill Ratcliffe *

Cover: Roberta Polfus

Index

This index is an alphabetical list of the important topics covered in this book. It will help you find information given in both words *and* pictures. To help you understand what an entry means, there is often a helping word in parentheses, for example, **barley** (cereal grass). If there is information in both words and pictures, you will see the words *(with pictures)* after the page number. If there is *only* a picture, you will see the word *(picture)* after the page number. If you do not find what you want in this index, please go to the General Index in Volume 15, which is a key to all of the books.